FRESH & HEALTHY

A Kirsty Melville Book

10

Ten Speed Press

PO Box 7123

Berkeley, California 94707

www.tenspeed.com

Packaged by

Media21 Publishing Pty Ltd

30 Bay Street, Double Bay, NSW 2028, Australia

First published by ACP Publishing Pty Ltd, Australia in 2000

Distributed in Canada by Ten Speed Press Canada

Library of Congress Cataloging-in-Publication Data
on file with the publisher.

ISBN #1-58008-392-7

Cover and text design by Michelle Wiener

First printing, 2002
Printed in China.

1 2 3 4 5 6 7 8 9 10—05 04 03 02 01

The Victor Chang Cardiac Research Institute

Fresh & Healthy was created in association with the Victor Chang Cardiac Research Institute of Australia. A pioneer of the modern era of heart transplantation, Victor Chang established the National Heart Transplant Unit at St. Vincent's Hospital in 1984. This unit has grown into the internationally renowned Victor Chang Cardiac Research Institute, which is now a leader in fundamental heart research, providing excellence in cardiovascular research and training, and in facilitating the rapid application of research discoveries to patient care.

Author's Acknowledgments

Behind every cookbook is a network of contributors just as vital to the book as the author. I was blessed to have a highly skilled and fun team behind the production of *Fresh & Healthy* that have made the book what it is. There are also others who helped and supported me during the process and I take this opportunity to express my sincere thanks to all involved.

To Stephen Balme, Philip Gore, Craig Osment, Sam, and all at Media 21—"The Producers", who were so great to work with. And to Loukie Werle, a very talented food writer who I was privileged to have patiently edit the copy.

To Alan Benson, my favorite photographer who can always turn my recipes into stunning delicious visions, and Michaela Le Compte for her beautiful styling work. Also thanks to Rodney Dunn for his behind the scenes work preparing the dishes for photography and Tyson Sadlo, Alan's assistant.

To my sister Wendy for her encouragement and support and for helping test a few of the recipes. And to all the taste testers—her family, Jaime, Andrew, and Stephanie and Robert Tsai, Dee, Andrew, Dane (my loyal teaser), and Elke Pierce, Jody, and Noel Parish and Kay and Norm Grant. Thanks for always being honest and enduring the retakes.

To my parents for putting up (smilingly) with a multitude of different flavors. When they'd really rather just eaten tomato sandwiches. And to God, for all the wonderful people and produce I had to work with.

Finally, and most importantly to me personally, to Stephen Andrews, a wonderful, patient, and caring man, who supported, encouraged, and nurtured me through the whole book from the other side of the world. And to his beautiful daughters, Samantha and Emily, who allowed him the time. Stephen brought to me a new dimension in food appreciation and recipe creation, reminding me of the significance of the social aspect of eating. In creating many of the recipes for him, I learned that one could go beyond their own personal boundaries with ease and discover new joys of playing with food when you think of someone else—that food should be social, fun, passionate, and not confined to recipes.

I personally dedicate this book, with my love and thanks, to Stephen, who is now my husband.

I hope you will feel free to expand your own boundaries with this book and personalize my recipes to bring yourselves and loved ones more pleasure, better health, and new discoveries.

Enjoy always—life is too short to deny yourself fun and pleasure.

FRESH & HEALTHY

Sally James

PHOTOGRAPHY BY ALAN BENSON

STYLING BY MICHAELA LE COMPTE

Ten Speed Press
Berkeley / Toronto

contents

introduction
by Deborah Madison
Author of *Vegetarian Cooking for Everyone* and *This Can't be Tofu!*

As the author of six (mostly) vegetarian cookbooks, it's often assumed that my interest is in healthy, low-fat cooking, but this isn't necessarily so. I was raised on a dairy farm and I love my cream and cheeses! While I do produce plenty of reasonable if not actual low-fat recipes, it's likely to be by accident. Or happy accident, I should say, because there are some foods that are just simply good and, it turns out, low in fat. A compote of blood oranges entwined with strips of their zest comes to mind. Not a trace of fat there. A caviar of scarlet Chioggia beets sharpened with vinegar and sweetened with pickled shallots, requires not a drop of oil to be good.

But in general, when a cookbook promises to deliver a battery of low-fat recipes, I'm pretty certain to look the other way, regardless of its promises of health or beauty. It's simply too dreary to contemplate a world without avocados, nuts, delicious oils in enough quantity to enjoy, pastry, and fresh mozzarella cheese. These usually forbidden foods aren't used excessively, but happily, they are present in *Fresh & Healthy*.

Sally James has what's rare—a sense of balance when it comes to healthy cooking. I was astonished to find macadamia nuts and their oil in a pumpkin soup (as well as a too-seldom-expressed appreciation of their nutritional qualities). Pine nuts and almonds show up in pastry shells. Avocados are included, as are olives. The tiramisu recipe actually looks good! Ms. James uses eggs in their entirety instead of pushing the yolks away as if they're some evil things. Huge quantities of sugar and starch don't take the place of fat, nor are carbohydrates eliminated. This is not extreme eating; it is good eating, and while it does ask you to give up some fats for the sake of your heart, the recipes are so pleasing to the eye as to perhaps make up for it. While I'm not sure I'll give up my delicate full-fat ricotta for the low-fat version, I might actually be convinced to try.

What's appealing to me about *Fresh & Healthy* is the underlying assumption that there's some equivalency between health and freshness. For me, it's freshness, more than low-fat ingredients that are the keys to healthy cooking, although oddly, the two meet, for true freshness implies locale and seasonality, which imply peak of flavor, and therefore the possibility of using less fats and sugar to make foods taste good. Fresh food should be good already. A ripe juicy peach doesn't need a crust and cream. That's healthful.

With the inclusion of whole grains along with lots of vegetables and fruits, and the tempered inclusion of those luxurious foods, such as avocados, macadamia nuts, and meat, the recipes in *Fresh & Healthy* really give the diet pyramid a workout. In doing so, they take the more practical middle path many of us imagine but seldom travel, between daily excesses and impossible-to-live-with regimens. Those seeking to improve their overall health will find that these are recipes they can live with.

eating fresh and healthy

A balanced, healthy diet combined with regular exercise is the best defense against heart disease by helping to regulate blood pressure, cholesterol, blood sugar, and body weight. A healthy lifestyle can be rewarding in more ways than just by making you feel better and reducing your chances of developing chronic disease. By applying a few healthy principles you can bring more pleasure into your daily life. There's no point in forcing yourself to eat a diet you hate and take up exercise that you dread—you'll never stick to it. The secret is to find healthy foods and exercise that you enjoy. Here are a few guidelines to help you find your own approach to healthy living.

enjoy a variety of foods

Aside from saving you from ultimate boredom, eating a wide variety of foods ensures you receive all the nutrients, including vitamins, minerals, antioxidants, and fiber, you need to live a healthy life. Here are a few tips:

- Vary the source of protein at each meal, and don't forget the seafood, bean, and other meatless options.
- Try new vegetables and fruits.
- Try some of the less used grains such as barley, couscous, wild rice, and quinoa.
- Explore the world of flavors in fresh herbs, spices, nuts, vinegars, mustards, virgin oils, and other fresh ingredients.

balance the food you eat with physical activity

In order to maintain or improve your weight as well as enhance your well-being, it's important to make sure you are physically active. Maintaining a healthy weight and active lifestyle is rewarding on many levels—you look and feel better, have less to carry around, have more energy, all the while reducing your risk of developing heart and blood vessel disease, late onset diabetes, and hypertension. Just find the right activity so that exercise is fun for you. Here's a start:

- Take time for a morning or evening walk, jog, or bike ride—on your own, to think, or as social event instead of meeting for coffee.
- Discover more active recreational activities for the weekend and vacations, even if it's just kicking around a soccer ball at a picnic, hiking, active gardening, or tossing a frisbee.
- Park further from your workplace and walk the distance.
- Don't forget to run and play with the dog (or borrow your neighbor's).
- Walk to destinations that are close by rather than relying on a car.

eat plenty of grain products, fruits, and vegetables

The bulk of your meals should include these important foods. They provide carbohydrates for energy, fiber, vitamins, minerals, and antioxidants (these are the elements in food which have been shown to improve resistance to heart disease and other degenerative diseases). And, they are filling, but not fattening. These delicious foods will also keep your meals varied and interesting.

Most grain foods, such as bread, rice, pasta, potatoes, cereals, and beans contain fiber, but there are different types in varying amounts. Soluble fiber found in oat products, legumes, barley, apples, and psyllium helps lower blood cholesterol and controls blood sugar levels. Insoluble fiber in whole-grain products, wheat bran, brown rice, and many fruit and vegetables, particularly in the skins, helps prevent and control bowel problems.

Eating meals based around a variety of these foods has long been linked to good health and is also very easy to do:

- Whether in a smoothie or just sliced over cereal, add a piece or two of fruit to your breakfast.
- Instead of the requisite meat and cheese, try a sandwich piled with ingredients such as tomato, cucumber, lettuce, and carrot.
- Make dinner more colorful with a stir-fry or grill a variety of vegetables, and cleanse your taste buds with simple, sliced fresh fruit.
- Experiment with different breads and grains during meals, and instead of relying on butter or mayonnaise as a spread, try dipping breads in extra virgin olive oil or spreading with avocado, cottage or ricotta cheese, mustard, chutney, or other lower-fat spreads.
- Snack on dried fruit and nuts, fresh fruit and juices.
- When you prepare pasta, make the pasta the focus, rather than the sauce.
- Design more meals based around the side dish, rather than a meat main course. Try meals centered around beans, lentils, or other mixed grains.

TEN EASY STEPS TO A HEALTHIER HEART

1. START EACH DAY WITH A POSITIVE ATTITUDE
The only way to make a habit of a healthy lifestyle is to wake up each morning believing that you are going to enjoy everything you eat and all of your activity for the day. Life is too short to force yourself to eat and do things that bring a grimace rather than a smile.

2. MAKE EATING A SOCIAL ACTIVITY
Rediscover the joy of family meals and have fun in the kitchen. Experiment with your family and friends with a new fruit, vegetable, or fish each week. Experiment with flavors using different herbs, seasonings, rice, breads, and pastas or try new international foods.

3. ADD COLOR TO YOUR PLATE
Make every meal as colorful as you can. Not only will it have more visual appeal, it's a great way to help you get a wide variety of nutrients, fiber, and flavor.

4. ENJOY HEALTHY FATS AND OILS
You don't have to give up fats and oils to have a healthy heart—just choose healthier oils and more nutritious sources of fat. Instead of butter on bread try dipping it in a fruity olive oil or spreading it with avocado. Grind nuts such as macadamias, hazelnuts, and almonds and use in cakes, cookies, and pastry instead of high-fat alternatives.

5. MOVE MORE
Whether it's walking, swimming, dancing, gardening, playing a sport, or just taking the dog for a walk, do more of it.

6. INCORPORATE FISH INTO YOUR DIET
Fish, especially salmon, tuna, mackerel, sardines, and trout, are full of the valuable, heart-friendly Omega-3 Fatty Acids. There's so much choice, you can eat fish four times a week and never be bored. It's also quick and easy to cook and is best simply served.

7. BECOME FRIENDS WITH YOUR DOCTOR
Have regular checkups as advised by your doctor— cholesterol, blood pressure, diabetes are all risk factors for heart disease.

8. ENJOY FINE WINES BY THE GLASS
Research shows that a glass of wine with dinner can lower your risk of heart disease. If you enjoy wine with meals, savor a good wine with a mineral water on the side—there has to be some reason why Europeans commonly pair these two and have a long history of healthy hearts.

9. FIND FLAVORS IN OTHER PLACES THAN THE SALT SHAKER
If you buy high-quality ingredients and use fresh herbs, vinegars, and other low-salt seasonings, you'll find the salt shaker will soon gather dust.

10. RELAX
Stress is not heart-friendly. Spoil yourself with time each day to unwind, relax, and pamper your mind and body.

TOOLS FOR A HEALTHY KITCHEN

KNIVES
A good set of sharp knives makes healthy cooking easier and faster. Trimming fat from meat and slicing vegetables for salsas will become a breeze!

PARCHMENT PAPER
Use parchment paper instead of fat to give baking dishes a nonstick surface.

NONSTICK PANS
These are invaluable for low-fat cooking, as little or no fat is required. Invest in good quality pans in a range of sizes to suit your own cooking needs. Remember to use wooden or plastic utensils, as metal will scratch the surface.

A WOK
If you do a lot of Asian cooking and stir-frying, a wok is essential. Nonstick woks are available and a good investment for the healthy cook.

A SLOTTED SPOON
These are great for lifting cooked foods from the cooking water, so you can reuse the water. Also ideal for lifting the fat off the surface of soups, casseroles, and stocks.

choose foods low in saturated fat

There are many reasons to reduce the amount of saturated fat you eat. High-fat diets tend to add weight because fat is calorie intensive and easily stored. And eating too much saturated fat tends to raise blood cholesterol levels—a major risk factor for developing heart and blood vessel disease.

There are three types of fats in food: saturated, monounsaturated, and polyunsaturated, and foods containing fat will have a mixture of these in varying amounts. Basically, you are better off choosing foods higher in monounsatured and polyunsatured fats, as they will help lower blood cholesterol. Just remember, they are all high in calories, so if you're watching your weight, go easy.

SATURATED FATS	MONOUNSATURATED FATS	POLYUNSATURATED FATS
butter and solid cooking margarines coconut oil and copha lard dairy fat in cream, cheese, ice cream, and sour cream meat fat chicken skin commercial cookies, cakes, and processed food that contain palm oil or hydrogenated oils pastries many fast foods	olive, peanut, and canola oil canola margarine macadamias, peanuts, hazelnuts, almonds, and cashews avocado	margarines like sunflower, safflower, soybean, corn, sesame, cottonseed, and grapeseed oils oils in fish, such as salmon, swordfish, mackerel, tuna, and trout walnuts and Brazil nuts seeds

Ways to reduce the saturated fat in your meals:

- Enjoy fish more often, and when you eat meat, choose lean cuts.
- Rely on tomato, vegetable, or wine-based sauces instead of cream and butter.
- Savor some of the richly flavored nut oils such as macadamia or hazelnut.
- Substitute low-fat dairy foods for high-fat ones. Try whipped sweetened ricotta instead of whipped cream, or fresh mozzarella on pizza and cheese plates rather than cheddar or jack.

moderate sugars and indulgences

Even though sugar is not the bad guy it was once said to be, sugary foods tend to have empty calories and should only be used as a treat, not as a meal replacement or regular snack. Foods high in sugar also often carry with them a load of fat, so read labels carefully.

Some low-sugar strategies:

- Sweeten desserts and cakes with fruit purée.
- Replace that bowl of sweets with dried fruit, nuts, and a few chocolate kisses thrown in.
- Instead of buying a whole block of chocolate, savor every bite of a single gourmet chocolate—quality versus quantity!
- Take some family kitchen time on weekends to bake a stock of homemade cookies like the ones in this book (see page 144). They'll have a whole lot less sugar, fat, and processed ingredients.

choose a diet moderate in salt and sodium

Eating too much salt can contribute to high blood pressure. Look for low or no salt foods and use fresh herbs, juices, and other flavorful ingredients so you don't need to rely on the salt shaker. Check out some of the flavor options in the back of the book for ideas on how to reduce salt and increase flavor.

healthy flavors

Once you embark on a healthy style of eating, a whole new world of flavors will gradually unfold, and you'll find that soon your tastes and preferences will change. The first few weeks and even months, however, can be a struggle as you attempt to find ways of reducing and improving the type of fat you use and yet still be satisfied by your meals. Many often give up at this stage, but take heart, there are a few secrets to creating meals that look and taste as good as they are for you.

The following are some tips for substituting commonly used foods high in saturated fat with more desirable ingredients that will give the dish the texture and flavors you are used to.

HIGH-FAT DAIRY FOODS

Dairy foods have an important place in a healthy diet—they are rich in calcium and contain protein and many vitamins and minerals. It's just a matter of choosing the lower-fat ones.

Cream can be replaced by evaporated skim milk in sauces and desserts, whipped cream with ricotta whipped with powdered sugar, vanilla, or fruit for serving with desserts. Sour cream is easily substituted with plain low-fat yogurt.

Cheeses are now available in a huge variety of reduced-fat options, but you need to read the label as the claims can be deceptive. For sandwiches, fruit plates, and on pizza try fresh mozzarella or reduced-fat mozzarella; crumble feta or ricotta on salads and pasta sauces; or choose an intensely flavored cheese such as Parmesan, of which just a few shavings are needed to top of a risotto or casserole.

Milk- and butter-based white sauces traditionally used for dishes such as pasta and vegetables can be made with skim milk or evaporated skim milk and thickened with corn flour. Fresh ricotta cheese is even nicer tossed through pasta for a creamy sauce.

Ice cream is perhaps the easiest change, with the realm of low-fat ice creams, sorbets, milk-based gelatos, and frozen yogurts available.

MEAT AND CHICKEN

Some people complain that lean meat or skinless chicken is hard to cook and can become tough and bland, but with a little care you can ensure a tender, juicy finished project. When broiling or barbecuing, marinate the meat first, sear on high heat, brush with a marinade while cooking, and take care not to overcook the meat.

Casseroles, soups, and stews can be low in fat just by using lean cuts of meat and trimming off fat before cooking. They can also be bulked up with beans and grains and, if you have time to chill casseroles, soups, and stews before serving, the fat will rise to the surface and can be lifted off.

DEEP-FRIED FOODS

Deep-frying is not the only way to make crisp french fries, crumbed fish, or crusty chicken. Brush or spray steamed potatoes and other root vegetables with a light coating of oil and bake in the oven. Coat fish and chicken in crumbs made from ground cereal flakes such as corn flakes before baking, or be adventurous and try ground nuts, herbs, polenta, or couscous as a crust.

PASTRY

Try using filo pastry for making rolls or cases for fruit desserts. You can brush every few sheets with oil or yogurt if you like, but it's also great just straight from the pack.

These are just a few ideas and, as you explore the world of simple healthy food, you'll find many of your own kitchen tricks. Above all, ENJOY.

Vegetable-Crusted Honey Prawns (page 12)

nibbles & starters

Vegetable-Crusted Honey Prawns

Serves 4

205 calories per serving; **7.5 g** total fat; **1.1 g** saturated fat; **535 mg** sodium

12 large prawns in shell
1 tablespoon honey
1 tablespoon thinly grated ginger
1 tablespoon plum sauce
1 teaspoon reduced-sodium soy sauce
1 carrot, peeled and thinly grated
1 large potato, peeled and thinly grated
1 tablespoon sesame seeds, plus
   1 teaspoon extra
1 tablespoon peanut or olive oil

Dipping Sauce

1 tablespoon oyster sauce
2 tablespoons rice wine or sherry
1 tablespoon lime or lemon juice

Preheat oven to 375°F.

Combine the dipping sauce ingredients and set aside.

Peel and devein the prawns leaving tails intact. Combine the honey, ginger, plum sauce, and soy sauce in a small bowl. In a separate flat bowl combine the carrot, potato, and sesame seeds. Holding the tails, dip the prawns in the honey mixture to coat well. Roll in the grated vegetables, pressing in well to hold crust in place.

Heat the oil in a nonstick or heavy-bottomed pan to high and sear the prawns for 10–15 seconds on both sides to brown the crust. Transfer to the oven and bake for 2–3 minutes or until prawns are opaque and firm. Take care not to bake too long or they will be tough.

Serve immediately, scattered with the extra sesame seeds, and with the dipping sauce.

Pork and Apple Wontons

Makes 25 wontons

120 calories per serving; **1.5 g** total fat; **0.4 g** saturated fat; **235 mg** sodium (note: fairly high in sodium)

Serve with soy sauce for dipping. For the leanest option, chop in a food processor to a coarse ground texture.

2 teaspoons peanut or olive oil
1 spring onion, chopped
6½ ounces ground pork
1 granny smith or other tart apple, grated
1 tablespoon currants
1 tablespoon plum sauce
1 tablespoon oyster or hoisin sauce
25 wonton wrappers
1 egg, beaten

Preheat the oven to 375°F.

Heat the oil in a nonstick pan, add the spring onion and cook for 2 minutes or until soft. Add the pork and cook, stirring, for 2–3 minutes then add the apple and cook until all meat is browned. Remove from heat and stir in the currants and sauces. Allow to cool slightly.

Lay a wonton wrapper on a clean dry surface with a corner facing you. Place about ½ tablespoon of the meat mixture in the center and brush the edges lightly with egg. Fold the bottom half over the top to make a triangle then bring the side corners together under the dumpling. Moisten with egg and pinch to hold in place. Repeat with remaining wontons. Place on lined baking sheets and bake for 10–15 minutes or until golden brown and crisp.

d Apple Wontons

Vegetable Antipasto

A platter for 6

330 calories per serving; **23 g** total fat; **6.6 g** saturated fat; **510 mg** sodium

2 red bell peppers, halved and seeded
2 cups diced pumpkin
3 cobs fresh corn, cut into 3 segments
¼ cup extra virgin olive oil
freshly ground pepper
4 small roma tomatoes, halved lengthwise
8 large leaves basil
4 small balls fresh mozzarella
12 spears asparagus
½ cup black olives
2 tablespoons lemon juice
¼ cup balsamic or red wine vinegar
¼ cup crumbled low-salt goat or feta cheese
¼ cup roughly chopped roasted
  hazelnuts or almonds

Preheat oven to 375°F.

Broil the pepper, skin side up, until the skin blackens. Place in a paper bag for 10 minutes then peel and slice. Lightly steam or microwave pumpkin until nearly cooked. Place on a lined roasting pan with the corn. Brush both with a little of the olive oil, season with pepper, and bake for 10–15 minutes or until pumpkin has become crisp and golden. Season the cut surface of the tomatoes with freshly ground pepper and top with a basil leaf and thick slice of mozzarella. Add to the roasting pan with the asparagus in the last 5–6 minutes of cooking, just until the cheese has melted and the asparagus is tender.

Purée the olives and lemon juice to make a coarse paste for spreading the bread, and whisk the remaining oil with the vinegar to make a dressing.

To serve, lay all the vegetables individually on a large platter. Scatter the cheese and nuts over the asparagus and drizzle all with the dressing.

Vietnamese Chicken and Mango Summer Rolls

Makes 8 rolls

160 calories per serving; **3.9 g** total fat; **0.7 g** saturated fat; **140 mg** sodium

juice of 1 lime
1 teaspoon fish sauce
1 teaspoon brown sugar
1 tablespoon rice wine or wine vinegar
2 cooked chicken breasts, shredded
1 tablespoon chopped fresh basil
1 tablespoon chopped fresh mint
1 spring onion, finely chopped
2 tablespoons sliced pickled ginger
4 by 6-inch rice papers
1 cup pea sprouts
1 mango, thinly sliced
cracked black pepper
¼ cup chopped roasted peanuts (optional)

Dipping sauce

juice of 1 lime
1 tablespoon rice wine or vinegar
1 tablespoon reduced-sodium soy sauce
1 tablespoon grated ginger

Combine dipping sauce ingredients and set aside. In a large bowl, whisk together the lime juice, fish sauce, sugar, and rice wine. Toss with the chicken, basil, and mint, cover and refrigerate for 20–30 minutes to allow flavors to develop. Stir in the onion and ginger.

Just before serving, soak a sheet of rice paper in warm water for about 20 seconds or until soft. Pat dry on each side with a clean tea towel. Lay sheet on a work surface and arrange some sprouts along the side closest to you, leaving a 1-inch border at the end. Top with about ¼ cup of the chicken mixture, then a few slices of mango and season with pepper. Sprinkle with peanuts then roll up, folding in the sides as you go. Place, seam side down, on a flat dish and cover with a damp tea towel. Repeat with remaining ingredients then refrigerate until ready to serve.

Serve the summer rolls whole or sliced in half diagonally, with the dipping sauce.

Pumpkin and Macadamia Nut Soup

Serves 4

245 calories per serving; **21 g** total fat; **3.1 g** saturated fat; **45 mg** sodium

1 tablespoon macadamia nut or olive oil
½ cup roughly chopped macadamia nuts
1 small white onion, chopped
1 teaspoon grated ginger
2 cups diced pumpkin
1 apple, peeled and chopped
3 cups chicken stock
whole or halved macadamia nuts, roasted,
  for garnish

Heat oil in a heavy-bottomed pan, add the macadamia nuts, onion, and ginger and sauté for 2–3 minutes, or until golden brown. Add the pumpkin and apple and cook 2–3 minutes then pour over the stock. Cover and simmer for 20 minutes or until pumpkin is soft. Transfer mixture to a blender and process until smooth and creamy.

Reheat and serve in large bowls with a few roasted macadamias tossed over for garnish.

Baked Scallop and Mushroom Soufflés

Makes 12 canapes

40 calories per serving; **2 g** total fat; **0.4 g** saturated fat; **40 mg** sodium

These are perfect accompaniments to a crisp, fruity, sparkling wine.

You need only a few dried mushrooms to deliver a powerful and exotic mushroom flavor. They can be quite expensive, but a little goes a long way. Store them in airtight jars in a cool and dark place and they'll keep well for a long time. Always soak well—length of time depends on thickness—and retain the soaking water to use later in soups or risottos.

15 mushrooms (make sure 12 of them are large enough to hold a scallop, and with a deep cup)
¼ cup dried sliced mushrooms
2 egg whites, lightly beaten
2 tablespoons fresh ricotta cheese
1 tablespoon chopped fresh basil
freshly ground pepper
12 scallops, without roe
olive oil for brushing tops
thyme sprigs, to garnish

Preheat oven to 350°F.

Remove the stems from 12 of the mushrooms. Finely dice the remaining 3. Soak the dried mushrooms in enough boiling water to cover for 10 minutes. Place in a saucepan with the chopped mushrooms and blanch until very soft. Drain well and press excess moisture out using paper towels. Place in a food processor with the egg whites, ricotta, basil, and pepper. Purée to a light mousse consistency. Spoon mixture into mushrooms and top with a scallop. Brush scallop with oil and bake for 8–10 minutes or until scallops are just cooked—they should still be plump and juicy.

Serve immediately, scattered with thyme sprigs.

Chive and Potato Cakes with Smoked Salmon and Beet Relish

Makes about 20

40 calories per cake; **1 g** total fat; **0.2 g** saturated fat; **170 mg** sodium

1 cup firm mashed potatoes

2 eggs

2 tablespoons low-fat yogurt

¼ cup low-fat milk

1 tablespoon snipped chives

freshly ground pepper

Beet relish

1 large beet, thinly grated

1 tablespoon lemon juice

2 teaspoons finely chopped ginger

Yogurt sauce

½ cup low-fat yogurt

1 tablespoon chopped fresh dill leaves or
2 teaspoons dried

To serve

6–8 slices gravlax or smoked salmon

Combine the beet relish ingredients and set aside.

To make the chive and potato cakes, combine all the ingredients and mix well. Heat a lightly oiled nonstick frying pan and place tablespoons of mixture in the pan. Cook for 1–2 minutes each side or until golden brown. Keep warm in a low oven while the remainder are cooked. Prepare these just before serving so they are still crisp and warm.

To make the yogurt sauce, combine the yogurt and dill and place a small amount on each cake.

To serve, cut gravlax into small strips and arrange on yogurt, then top with the beet relish. Serve immediately.

Fresh Corn Soup with Crab Salsa

Serves 6

135 calories per serving; **3.5 g** total fat; **0.8 g** saturated fat; **360 mg** sodium

5 cobs corn (about 3 cups)

2 teaspoons olive oil

2 green onions, chopped

2 teaspoons grated ginger

1½ cups chicken stock

2 tablespoons chopped fresh cilantro

1 cup low-fat milk

white pepper and lemon juice

Crab Salsa

½ cup crab meat

1 roma tomato, seeded and diced

1 tablespoon chopped cilantro, plus extra

1 tablespoon lemon juice

Combine all the ingredients for the salsa and refrigerate until ready to use.

To make the soup, cook the whole corn on the cob, then cool slightly and remove corn kernels. Heat the oil in a large saucepan, add the green onions and ginger and saute for 1–2 minutes or until they start to soften. Set aside ½ cup of the corn and add the remainder to the saucepan with the chicken stock and cilantro. Bring to a boil and cook for 5 minutes.

Purée in a blender until smooth. Return to the pan, add the milk and reserved corn and season to taste with pepper and lemon juice. Reheat and serve with a spoon of the crab salsa.

White Bean, Leek, and Celery Soup with Parmesan Croutons

Serves 4

365 calories per serving; **9 g** total fat; **2.1 g** saturated fat; **840 mg** sodium

Try making your own chicken stock using leftover cuts and bones of chicken. Skim off the fat, boil to concentrate, and store in ice cube trays. Not only will the flavor be a lot better, it will contain considerably less salt.

If preferred, you can use dried beans. Soak overnight then cook for 20–30 minutes before adding to soup. This would further reduce the salt content.

1 slice lean bacon, all fat trimmed

4 cups chicken stock (see note)

1 leek, white part only, washed and sliced

1 red onion, chopped

1 clove garlic, crushed, optional

3 stalks celery, sliced

1 large carrot, thinly sliced

1 sprig thyme or oregano

1 bay leaf

12-ounce can white or navy beans, drained and well rinsed (see note)

cracked black pepper

Parmesan croutons

12 diagonal slices sourdough or woodfired baguette

1 tablespoon olive oil

cracked black pepper

1 tablespoon grated parmesan cheese

In a large saucepan, heat the bacon until it starts to brown and crisp. Drain away any fat and add a few spoons of the stock, the leek, onion, garlic, celery, and carrot. Cook over a low heat until vegetables start to soften. Add the remaining ingredients and bring to a boil. Cover and simmer for 20–30 minutes or until vegetables are very tender and soup is aromatic. Season to taste with cracked pepper and serve with parmesan croutons or just some crusty bread.

To make croutons, preheat the oven to 325°F. Brush bread with olive oil, season with pepper, and sprinkle with the parmesan cheese. Place on a baking sheet and bake until golden brown and crisp, about 10 minutes.

Tortilla Cones with Tuna Tartare

Makes 20

35 calories per cone; **1.5 g** total fat; **0.3 g** saturated fat; **20 mg** sodium

Cut the leftover tortilla scraps into shapes and bake to use as healthy chips with a dip or just to nibble on.

The longer the fish is left to marinate, the more it will 'cook' in the bowl.

2 large flour tortillas or
4–5 small tortillas

Tuna Tartare

4 ounces fresh tuna, finely diced (you could also use fresh salmon, swordfish, snapper, or kingfish)

1 spring onion, finely chopped

1 roma tomato, seeded and finely diced

2 teaspoons extra virgin olive oil

juice of 2 limes

¼ cup finely chopped cilantro

1 red chile, finely chopped (or use Tabasco)

¼ cup finely diced avocado

2 tablespoons low-fat yogurt

Cut tortillas into rounds using a cookie cutter (see note).

Make a slit from the middle to the outside of each round and shape into cones, securing with a toothpick. Place on a baking sheet and bake for 8–10 minutes or until browned and crisp. Carefully remove toothpick and cool on a wire rack. These can be made a few days ahead of time and kept in an airtight container.

To make tuna tartare, combine all ingredients except the avocado and yogurt, cover, and chill for at least 1 hour or overnight (see note).

Just before serving, drain away excess juice and gently fold in the avocado and yogurt. Spoon mixture inside cones and serve immediately.

Avocado and Choyote Squash Soup

Serves 2

175 calories per serving; **15 g** total fat; **3.4 g** saturated fat; **50 mg** sodium

Serve with an extra dollop of yogurt and a sprinkling of snipped chives or chopped flat-leaf parsley.

1 large choyote squash, peeled and diced

1¼ cups vegetable or chicken stock

½ large or 1 small avocado

1–2 teaspoons lemon juice

white pepper

1 tablespoon plain low-fat yogurt (optional)

Boil the squash in the stock for 10 minutes or until tender. Transfer to a blender with the stock and remaining ingredients and purée until smooth. Reheat and serve immediately.

Chilled Asparagus Bisque

Serves 4

50 calories per serving; **0.5 g** total fat; **0.2 g** saturated fat; **60 mg** sodium

Serve with some fresh cilantro, and extra dollops of yogurt, if desired, and some chewy sourdough bread.

When buying green asparagus, look for crisp, shiny stems, with tightly closed tips. To remove the woody bottoms, just hold the stem with both hands and bend. The woody bit will simply snap off. Green asparagus don't need peeling, whereas white asparagus do. Purple asparagus are best left uncooked and used in salads.

1 onion, peeled and diced
3 stalks celery, chopped
2 teaspoons thyme
2½ cups chicken stock
1 pound fresh asparagus, woody stalks removed and chopped
¼ cup low-fat natural yogurt
lemon juice and white pepper

In a large saucepan, blanch the onion, celery, and thyme in a little of the stock until onion is translucent. Add the asparagus and remaining stock and bring to a boil. Cover and simmer for 10 minutes. Pour mixture into a blender, add yogurt and purée until smooth. If the asparagus is stringy, you may need to pass the mixture through a sieve. Season to taste with lemon and pepper and chill.

Mustard Pepper Salmon with Red Wine Sauce (page 30)

fish & seafood

Mustard Pepper Salmon with Red Wine Sauce

Serves 4

220 calories per serving; **7.5 g** total fat; **1.5 g** saturated fat; **70 mg** sodium

2 large or 4 small zucchini

4 (5-ounce) fillets fresh salmon

1 tablespoon freshly ground pepper

1 tablespoon mustard seeds

2 teaspoons oregano

2 teaspoons extra virgin olive oil

½ cup red wine

4–6 large fresh leaves basil

Boil or microwave the whole zucchini until just cooked through. Allow to cool enough to slice into thin strips. Set aside.

Remove the skin and bones from the salmon. Combine the pepper, mustard seeds, and oregano and press into the salmon to coat. Heat the oil in a nonstick pan and cook the salmon for 1–2 minutes on each side. Transfer to a baking dish and keep warm in a very low oven.

Pour the red wine into the pan and cook until the wine reduces and thickens. Return the zucchini strips to a separate saucepan with a little water or stock and the basil and reheat. Serve the salmon over the zucchini and spoon over the red wine sauce.

Pan-Seared Calamari Ponzu with Endives

Serves 4 as an appetizer

220 calories per serving; **6 g** total fat; **1.1 g** saturated fat; **670 mg** sodium

For a more complete meal, you can serve this with 2 cups cooked hot steamed rice.

3–4 calamari tubes, about 1 pound altogether

2 teaspoons olive oil

1 tablespoon sweet soy sauce

1 tablespoon each lime and lemon juice
  (or just use one)

⅓ cup pickled ginger, sliced

2 teaspoons sesame seeds

1 tablespoon rice wine vinegar

few drops sesame oil

2 cups pea sprouts

2 endives, thinly sliced horizontally

Cut the calamari into thick slices and turn inside out. Heat a heavy-bottomed pan and add oil. Sauté calamari for 30 seconds, add the sweet soy sauce, juices, and ginger. Cook for 1 minute. Remove calamari and keep warm. Reduce sauce to a glaze.

While sauce is reducing, toast the sesame seeds in a nonstick pan. While hot add the rice wine vinegar, sesame oil, sprouts, and endives. Toss quickly then remove from heat. Serve calamari over the vegetables and serve immediately.

Pan-Seared Calamari Ponzu with Endive

Lemongrass Crab on Spaghettini

Serves 4

570 calories per serving; **6 g** total fat; **1.3 g** saturated fat; **325 mg** sodium

For a crunchy topping, try crushing some Japanese rice crackers in a plastic bag using a rolling pin and sprinkling over at the last minute.

Wakame is dried seaweed strips which swell up and soften when soaked. You can find it in most Asian and health food stores.

For lovers of heat, a teaspoon of hot chile sauce in the crab can work well, but I find it can mask the subtle aromas of the lemongrass and lime.

1 pound spaghettini

2 tablespoons wakame (see note)

1 kaffir lime leaf (optional)

8 thick spears asparagus, trimmed and chopped into 3 equal pieces

Lemongrass Crab

2 teaspoons olive or peanut oil

1 stalk lemongrass, bruised and finely chopped, white part only

1 tablespoon grated fresh ginger

13 ounces fresh crab meat (or use premium canned chunk style, rinsed)

juice and grated zest of 1 lime

2 tablespoons rice wine, or dry white wine

2 tablespoons light coconut milk

Place the spaghettini in a large pot of rapidly boiling water with the wakame and lime leaf and cook according to directions on the package. Add the chopped asparagus in final 30 seconds of cooking. Drain, remove leaf, and keep warm.

Meanwhile, heat the oil in a nonstick pan, add the lemongrass and ginger, and cook for 2 minutes or until they start to soften and brown. Add the crab and cook, stirring for 1 minute. Pour in the lime juice and zest, rice wine, and coconut milk, cover and steam for 2–3 minutes or until heated through and aromatic. Serve immediately on the hot pasta.

Cilantro and Tomato Seafood Bake with Wild Rice Pilaf

Serves 4

395 calories per serving; **14 g** total fat; **2.7 g** saturated fat; **400 mg** sodium

Serve with Italian bread and salad.

Wild rice is not actually rice at all: it's an aquatic grass with a delicious nutty flavor. The most expensive has long, glossy grains, but cheaper varieties, which may contain broken grains, are fine for many uses —stuffing poultry, for instance. In cooking, the outer covering may open, revealing the inner white grain, and the grains may swell three to four times their initial volume. Don't confuse this rice with Thai black rice, which is glutinous and is frequently used for sweet dishes.

1 tablespoon olive oil

1 tablespoon chopped ginger

½ cup chopped leek

1 stalk celery or fennel, chopped

⅓ cup dry white wine

12-ounce can chopped Italian tomatoes

½ cup chopped cilantro

1 (10-ounce) fillet fresh salmon, skin and bones removed (or any firm–fleshed fish)

8 king prawns, peeled with tails in tact

12 plump scallops

2 tablespoons grated parmesan

Wild Rice Pilaf

⅔ cup pure wild rice

2 green onions, chopped

1 carrot, grated

2 tablespoons chopped parsley

juice and grated rind of ½ lemon

¼ cup roasted slivered almonds

Preheat oven to 325°F.

To make the pilaf, place the rice in a pan of boiling water and cook for 5 minutes. Turn off the heat, cover with a tight-fitting lid and steam for 20–30 minutes or until rice begins to split and curl. Return to a boil and cook for 5–10 minutes or until tender. Drain, rinse, and return to the pan with the onions, carrot, parsley, lemon juice, and rind. Keep warm.

While rice cooks, heat the oil in a frying pan and sauté the ginger, leek, and celery for 2–3 minutes or until soft. Add the wine and tomatoes and bring to a boil. Add the cilantro and remove from heat.

Cut the salmon into ½-inch thick slices and place with the prawns and scallops in a casserole dish. Pour over the tomato mixture and bake for 10–15 minutes or until fish just starts to flake but is still pink inside. Just before serving, toss the almonds through the rice and serve with the fish spooned over. Sprinkle with the parmesan cheese.

Grilled Whiting Fillets with Caper Salsa

Serves 4

265 calories per serving; **13 g** total fat; **2 g** saturated fat; **250 mg** sodium

To seed and dice the tomatoes, insert a fork into the stem end and plunge tomato into boiling water for 30 seconds. Run under cool water then slip the skin off and cut tomato in half. Remove seeds and dice.

1¼ pounds small whiting or garfish fillets, boned and scaled, skin on
olive oil, to brush
cracked black pepper

Vinaigrette

2 tablespoons extra virgin olive oil
2 tablespoons red wine vinegar
1 tablespoon lemon juice
1 tablespoon chopped flat-leaf parsley

Caper Salsa

3 vine-ripened tomatoes, seeded and diced (see note)
1 cucumber, seeded and diced
½ red onion, diced
2 tablespoons capers, rinsed and drained
½ green bell pepper, finely diced
arugula leaves, to serve

Whisk together the vinaigrette ingredients.

Just before cooking the fish, combine the diced tomato, cucumber, onion, capers, and bell pepper in a bowl, gently toss with the dressing.

Brush the whiting lightly with oil and place, skin side down, on a baking sheet. Put under a broiler and cook 2–3 minutes only or until flesh just starts to flake.

To serve, spread the arugula on a platter, top with salsa, arrange fillets in circular fashion on top, and season to taste with cracked pepper.

Chile Prawns on Angel Hair Pasta

Serves 4

295 calories per serving; **4 g** total fat; **0.6 g** saturated fat; **715 mg** sodium

1 pound angel hair pasta
1½ pounds prawns
2 teaspoons extra virgin olive oil
1 red chile, thinly sliced
1 clove garlic, finely chopped
2 spring onions, chopped
2 tablespoons fruity dry white wine
1 teaspoon reduced-sodium soy sauce
1 teaspoon sweet chile sauce
2 roma tomatoes, seeded and diced
¼ cup roughly chopped fresh basil
¼ cup roughly chopped fresh cilantro
1 tablespoon wine vinegar

Cook pasta according to directions and keep warm.

Peel and devein prawns leaving tails intact. Heat the oil in a large nonstick pan or heavy-bottomed pan and sauté the chile and garlic for 1 minute. Add the spring onions and prawns and cook until prawns start to curl and turn opaque. Add the wine and sauces and cook for 2 minutes or until mixture comes to a boil. Toss with the tomato, herbs, and vinegar, remove from heat and serve immediately spooned around the cooked hot pasta.

Pan-Seared Lime Fish with a Warm Vegetable Salad

Serves 4

275 calories per serving; **14 g** total fat; **1.5 g** saturated fat; **175 mg** sodium

If you've never had much luck cooking fish, and would like to be eating more of it, as we all should, here is a simple, tasty, and foolproof dish that will work with just about any fish. My favorites this way are blue eye, mahi mahi, swordfish, and ocean trout. Be creative and experiment with your own blend of herbs and flavors. This is also great tossed through a salad or with a bowl of couscous. Try with the Cucumber Raita on page 108.

4 (5-ounce) fillets blue eye of other firm-fleshed fish, skin removed
freshly ground pepper
1 tablespoon cilantro, oregano, or
   tarragon leaves, or herbs of your choice
2 teaspoons olive oil
juice of 1 lime
¼ cup white wine
1 tablespoon balsamic or wine vinegar

Salad

1 large carrot, cut into long batons
12 green beans or 1 bunch fresh
   asparagus, halved
8–10 cherry tomatoes, halved
1 cucumber, sliced
arugula or mixed lettuce leaves
¼ cup flaked toasted almonds (optional)

Dressing

1 tablespoon olive oil
1 tablespoons lime juice
1 teaspoon grain mustard

Season the fish with the pepper and herbs to taste. Heat the oil in a nonstick pan and sear the fish for 1 minute until crisp and browned. Turn over and add the lime, wine, and vinegar to the pan. Cook for 2–3 minutes, or until fish just starts to flake when pressed with a fork. The cooking time will vary according to type and thickness of the fish. Just take care not to go past the 'just starting to flake' stage or it will become tough and less tender. Serve immediately over the warm vegetable salad and drizzle with pan juices.

To make the Warm Vegetable Salad, blanch the carrots for 2–3 minutes or until tender-crisp, then add the asparagus and blanch for 30 seconds. Toss with the remaining salad ingredients.

To make the dressing, combine the oil, lime juice, and mustard and toss with the salad.

Citrus Soy Snapper on Cucumber and Pickle Stir-Fry

Serves 4

400 calories per serving; **8 g** total fat; **1.6 g** saturated fat; **315 mg** sodium

finely chopped zest and the juice of 1 lemon

finely chopped zest and the juice of 1 orange

1 green onion, finely chopped

1 tablespoon reduced-sodium soy sauce

1 tablespoon brown sugar

1 tablespoon olive oil

4 (5-ounce) snapper fillets

2 cups cooked hot steamed jasmine rice

Cucumber and Pickle Stir-Fry

1 cucumber

1 large carrot

¼ cup pickled ginger

1 packet pea sprouts (or mung bean)

Preheat oven to 375°F.

Combine lemon and orange zest and onion and set aside.

Combine juices, soy sauce and brown sugar in a small saucepan and simmer until it starts to thicken. Add the zest mixture. Cook for another minute, remove from heat, add the olive oil, and allow to cool.

Brush the mixture onto one side of the snapper fillets and bake, crust side up, for 8–10 minutes.

Meanwhile, cut the cucumber and carrot into thin strips using a peeler, and stir-fry for 1 minute. Toss with the ginger and sprouts and heat through for 1 minute. Serve fish with steamed jasmine rice and stir-fry.

Tea-Smoked Flathead with Lemon Vinaigrette

Serves 4

320 calories per serving; **20 g** total fat; **4.2 g** saturated fat; **185 mg** sodium

Serve with baguettes or crusty bread.

3 tablespoons Earl Grey tea-leaves (or try Green Tea, Jasmine, or Lady Grey)

4 (5-ounce) flathead fillets, deboned and each cut into 3–4 strips

1 ripe avocado

1 head curly endive

Dressing

juice of 1 lemon

1 teaspoon mild dijon mustard

1 tablespoon extra virgin olive oil

freshly ground pepper

Whisk together the dressing ingredients and set aside.

Place tea-leaves in a heavy-bottomed pan or wok with a small rack inside. Place over a high heat and lay fillets on rack. Cover tightly with lid and smoke for 5 minutes. To help reduce the smoke entering the room, saturate a tea towel and wrap it around the lid seal. Remove from heat and allow to cool.

Slice the avocado finely and toss with some of the dressing. Arrange curly endive leaves on plates, top with the avocado and arrange fillets on top. Spoon over the dressing and serve immediately.

Prawn, Macadamia Nut, and Cilantro Ravioli

Serves 4 as a large entree or light meal

380 calories per serving; **8.5 g** total fat; **1.2 g** saturated fat; **1310 mg** sodium (note: high in salt, omit fish sauce if desired)

The macadamia nut, has taken the world by storm and not least because of its delicious buttery flavor and crisp texture. These nuts are a great source of fiber as well as oil, which is 78 per cent unsaturated—mainly mono-unsaturated—making it a healthy addition to our diet, when eaten in moderation. Macadamia nuts are expensive, so treat them with due respect. Buy in airtight packaging, and once opened, store in the refrigerator. Their high oil content makes them prone to rancidity.

¼ cup roasted macadamia nuts, roughly chopped

1 cup fresh cilantro leaves, reserve 24 leaves for the ravioli

1 tablespoon rice wine vinegar

1 tablespoon lime juice

freshly ground pepper

24 large king prawns, peeled

24 wonton wrappers

1 tablespoon reduced-sodium soy sauce

Stock

3 cups water

1 cup white wine

1 tablespoon fish sauce

1 kaffir lime leaf

1 stalk lemongrass, crushed and chopped

1 knob ginger, chopped

Bring the stock ingredients to a boil in a large saucepan.

In a small bowl combine the macadamia nuts, cilantro, vinegar, lime juice, and pepper to taste. Stir in the prawns. Lay out 12 of the wonton wrappers and place a spoonful of the mixture with 1 prawn on the center of each wrapper, topped with 2 cilantro leaves. Brush edges with water or beaten egg. Place another wonton wrapper on top, pressing edges to seal. Gently slide a few at a time in the boiling stock and cook 2–3 minutes or until prawns show bright orange through the dough. Remove with a slotted spoon and keep warm while remainder are cooked.

Strain a cup of the stock into a jug and mix in the soy sauce. Serve ravioli on shallow dishes or bowls and spoon some of the sauce over the top.

New Orleans Fish Cakes

Serves 4 as a main dish

355 calories per serving; **9 g** total fat; **2.4 g** saturated fat; **925 mg** sodium

As crab meat can be expensive, I've adapted the traditional crab cake recipe to include a mixture of fish and crab. Feel free to use all crab or all fish if you prefer.

Serve with a garden salad, vegetables, or sesame buns

If you'd like a sauce, try with yogurt and lime juice or the Tomato Salsa with the Octopus Salad on page 50.

7 ounces crab meat

10 ounces boneless white fish—try gemfish, flake, or ling, or ask your fishmonger

2 eggs

2 cups soft fresh bread crumbs

ground black pepper

cayenne pepper

1 tablespoon low-fat mayonnaise

2 teaspoons grain mustard

1 tablespoon fresh thyme leaves

¼ cup chopped parsley

1 teaspoon paprika

1 red onion, finely diced

½ cup chopped celery

2 teaspoons reduced-sodium Worcestershire sauce

tabasco sauce

grated zest and juice of ½ lime

2 teaspoons olive oil

Preheat oven to 375°F.

Place the crab, fish, and eggs in a food processor and process to a coarse paste. Set aside 1 cup of the bread crumbs and season to taste with pepper and cayenne. Add remaining ingredients, except the oil, to the fish and pulse on and off until just combined. Do not over mix. Shape mixture into cakes and roll in the seasoned bread crumbs.

Heat oil in a nonstick pan and cook fish cakes for 1–2 minutes on each side or until brown and crisp. Transfer to a parchment paper lined baking sheet and finish cooking in the oven for 6–8 minutes or until cooked and heated through.

Flaked Trout Bagels

Makes 4 bagels

345 calories per serving; **4.5 g** total fat; **1.1 g** saturated fat; **605 mg** sodium

If you find it too hard to eat the fish enclosed in the bagel, use the top to scoop up the juices as you go along.

1 large rainbow trout
½ cup low-fat milk
1 kaffir lime leaf (optional)
1 tablespoon chopped lemongrass
4 bagels
arugula or mixed lettuce leaves
freshly ground pepper
1 tablespoon capers

Dressing
½ cup low-fat yogurt
1 tablespoon fresh dill leaves
½ cucumber, grated
1 tablespoon lemon juice

Place trout, milk, lime leaf, and lemongrass in a frying pan with a lid and bring to a boil. Reduce heat and simmer for 8–10 minutes, turning once, until flesh just flakes. Remove fish and allow to cool. When cool, lift off skin, and remove flesh from the bones. Flake the flesh and refrigerate until ready to use.

Combine the dressing ingredients and mix well. Warm bagels in foil in the oven, split, and top with arugula leaves. Arrange flaked trout over leaves, season to taste with pepper and spoon over dressing and capers.

Spring Roll-Wrapped Ocean Trout

Serves 4

295 calories per serving; **6.5 g** total fat; **1.5 g** saturated fat; **600 mg** sodium

Wasabi, Japanese horseradish, is very hot. Only a little is needed. Too much and your sinuses will be cleared in an instant!

Bone-removing tip —believe it or not, eyebrow tweezers or any flat tipped tweezers are ideal.

4 fresh ocean trout fillets (swordfish, salmon, and tuna are also perfect)
2 tablespoons low-fat yogurt
½ teaspoon wasabi (see note)
1 teaspoon lime juice
4 sheets nori (seaweed sheets)
4 large spring roll wrappers
1 egg white, lightly beaten
1 teaspoon peanut or olive oil

Salad
1 tablespoon sweet soy sauce
1 tablespoon lime juice
few drops sesame oil
¼ cup pickled ginger, sliced
2 endives, leaves separated
½ red onion, thinly sliced

Remove skin and bones from ocean trout (see note). Combine the yogurt, wasabi, and lime and brush over the fish. Wrap each fillet in a nori sheet then in a spring roll wrapper, sealing edges with the egg white.

Combine the soy sauce, lime juice, and sesame oil for the salad and toss with the ginger, lettuce, and onion. Arrange on plates.

Heat the oil in a nonstick pan and sear the fillets over a medium heat for 2–3 minutes each side or until browned and crisp. Fish should still be pink inside. Cut diagonally in half and place over salad.

Roasted Swordfish with Crisp Calamari

Serves 4

350 calories per serving; **19 g** total fat; **3.8 g** saturated fat; **610 mg** sodium

Serve with steamed rice or cellophane noodles.

Swordfish is popular in the Mediterranean, especially on and around the island of Sicily, where, together with tuna, it is the mainstay of the healthy Mediterranean diet. Usually available in steaks—the fish is too large to fillet—the flesh resembles that of tuna and marlin, but is much lighter in color than those two. Cook this fish only lightly, because it can become dry when overcooked.

1 small fennel bulb
grated rind and juice of 1 lemon
1 tablespoon olive oil
4 (5-ounce) swordfish steaks
freshly ground pepper
1 medium tube calamari, very thinly sliced, to make about ¾ cup
1 tablespoon sesame seeds
1 tablespoon reduced-sodium soy sauce

Preheat oven to 375°F.

Remove the tough or blemished outer leaves of the fennel and slice the white root finely. Toss with the lemon rind and half of the juice and oil. Place over the base of one large or 4 small lightly oiled ovenproof dishes. Lay swordfish fillets over the fennel and season to taste with pepper. Toss the calamari with the remaining juice and oil, sesame seeds, and soy sauce. Spoon over the top of the swordfish and spread to cover the fillets. Bake for 15 minutes, or until swordfish just starts to flake but is still plump and tender.

Lightly steam the spinach until the leaves are just wilted. Keep warm. Place fish under a hot broiler for 1 minute to crisp the calamari and serve immediately.

Rice with Prawns and Wine

Serves 4

515 calories per serving; **6.5 g** total fat; **1.2 g** saturated fat; **600 mg** sodium

Serve with a large green salad.

1 tablespoon olive oil

2 spring onions, chopped

1 clove garlic, crushed

1½ cups arborio rice

1 cup dry white or sparkling wine

4 cups hot degreased chicken stock

1¼ pounds raw prawns, peeled, leaving tails intact

½ cup chopped fresh herbs (try cilantro, basil, parsley, tarragon)

grated rind and juice of 1 lemon

Heat oil in a heavy-bottomed large saucepan. Add the onion and garlic and cook for 1–2 minutes or until soft. Add the rice and cook, stirring for 1–2 minutes. Pour in the wine and cook until all liquid is absorbed. Pour in the stock, cover loosely, and cook for 15–20 minutes or until most of liquid is absorbed.

Add the prawns, fresh herbs, and lemon rind and juice, cover and cook on a low heat for 2–3 minutes or until prawns are opaque and cooked through. Remove from heat and let sit for 5 minutes before serving.

Slow-Cooked Octopus and Arugula Salad

Serves 6 as a light meal

180 calories per serving; **7.5 g** total fat; **1.2 g** saturated fat; **270 mg** sodium

I can't resist a wood-fired or sourdough loaf with this dish, but it is also great with a big dish of cooked pasta.

1¼ pounds baby octopus, cleaned

½ cup balsamic vinegar

½ cup white wine

6–8 leaves basil

2 cloves garlic, crushed

Salad

3 roma tomatoes, seeded and diced

1 red onion, finely diced

2–3 leaves basil

2 tablespoons extra virgin olive oil

freshly ground pepper

1 large bunch arugula

Preheat the oven to 325°F.

Remove the eyes and beak from the octopus if the fishmonger hasn't done so already. Place in large casserole dish and pour in the balsamic vinegar, wine, basil, and garlic. Cover and bake for 40–45 minutes or until octopus is very tender. Remove from liquid.

Combine the tomatoes, onion, basil, oil, and 1–2 tablespoons of the cooking liquid from the octopus. Toss well to combine and season to taste with pepper.

To serve, place arugula leaves on plates, top with the octopus and salad.

Squid Ink Pasta with Swordfish Ceviche

Serves 4

655 calories per serving; **14 g** total fat; **2.7 g** saturated fat; **300 mg** sodium

You could also use tuna, blue eye, or salmon—but not frozen. Look for firm, shiny fish, not sitting on or scattered with ice, and with no brownish hue.

12 ounces very fresh swordfish

2 tablespoons mirin (rice wine) or white wine

juice and zest of 1 lime

1 tablespoon extra virgin olive oil

2 teaspoons reduced-sodium soy sauce

¼ cup chopped fresh cilantro

¼ cup chopped fresh basil

1 pound squid ink fettuccine or preferred pasta (try spinach or tomato for the color)

Remove the skin from the swordfish and dice the flesh finely. Place in a bowl with the mirin, lime juice and zest, oil, soy sauce, cilantro, and basil. Cover, refrigerate, and allow to marinate for 20–30 minutes. Swordfish will begin to 'cook' in the marinade.

Meanwhile, cook the pasta according to directions, drain well, and return to pan. Toss through the swordfish ceviche. Allow to sit for a minute over a low heat, then serve while hot. Alternatively, serve pasta with ceviche spooned over the top. Enjoy with a mixed lettuce salad and tomatoes.

Caramelized Scallops on Warm Asparagus and Tomato Salad

Serves 4

110 calories per serving; **4.5 g** total fat; **0.7 g** saturated fat; **195 mg** sodium

This dish was inspired by a memorable meal by chef Robert Curry at Domaine Chandon Vineyards in California's Napa Valley.

1 bunch fresh asparagus, sliced diagonally

1 carrot, peeled, diagonally sliced

2 green onions, sliced into ½-inch thick pieces

5 tablespoons chicken stock

cracked black pepper

2 roma tomatoes, sliced

1 teaspoon brown sugar

2 teaspoons red wine vinegar

2 teaspoons extra virgin olive oil

24 plump scallops

Dressing

¼ cup vegetable or chicken stock

1 canned artichoke

1 teaspoon extra virgin olive oil

1 tablespoon lemon juice

Preheat oven to 400°F. Place the asparagus, carrots, onions, and stock in a small pan. Season to taste with cracked pepper and bring to a boil. Cook 2–3 minutes or until vegetables are tender. Stir in the tomatoes and keep warm.

Dissolve the sugar in the vinegar and set aside. Heat a frying pan with an ovenproof handle and add the oil. Season scallops on both sides with pepper and sear in hot pan for 1 minute. Add the sugared vinegar, rotate pan to distribute the liquid, and place in the oven for 2 minutes. Turn the scallops over then remove from pan.

Place the vegetables in the center of 4 warm plates, allowing the stock to spread out. Surround with 6 scallops and serve the dressing on the side.

To make the dressing, heat the chicken stock and boil the artichoke for 2–3 minutes. Place in a blender and purée, gradually adding the oil and lemon juice.

Grilled Veal with Orange and Rosemary Sauce (page 56)

meat

Grilled Veal with Orange and Rosemary Sauce

Serves 4

175 calories per serving; **4.5 g** total fat; **1 g** saturated fat; **120 mg** sodium

Serve with rice or pasta and steamed green beans, squash, and carrots, or vegetables of your choice.

2 teaspoons olive oil

4 (4-ounce) lean thick veal steaks

Sauce

¼ cup orange juice

¼ cup white wine

¼ cup chicken stock

1 sprig rosemary

freshly ground pepper

Heat a nonstick pan, add the oil, and sear the steaks for 2–3 minutes on each side or as desired. Transfer to a dish, cover with foil, and keep warm in a low oven. Add the juice, wine, stock, and rosemary to the pan and cook until mixture is a sauce consistency. Remove the rosemary and season to taste with pepper. Slice the veal and serve with the sauce spooned over.

Pork Balls with Noodles

Serves 4

580 calories per serving; **11 g** total fat; **3.3 g** saturated fat; **315 mg** sodium

If you can't find ground pork, buy diced pork or pork steak, trim off any fat and cut into small pieces. Place in a food processor with the egg, soy sauce, cilantro, and ginger and pulse on and off until ground. You could also try using chicken or ground veal.

1 pound lean ground pork (see note)

1 egg white, lightly whisked

2 teaspoons reduced-sodium soy sauce

2 tablespoons chopped fresh cilantro leaves
  (or 2 teaspoons dried leaves)

1 tablespoon thinly grated ginger

2 tablespoons cornstarch

2 cups degreased chicken stock

1 teaspoon fish sauce

4 green onions, ends trimmed and cut into
  2-inch batons

4 mushrooms

1 cup snow or snap peas

1 carrot, sliced

2 packages fresh udon noodles

Combine the ground meat, egg white, soy sauce, cilantro, and ginger in a bowl. Shape into small balls and toss in the cornstarch to coat. Bring the chicken stock and fish sauce to a boil in a large saucepan. Reduce heat to a simmer and add the pork balls. Cook for 10 minutes or until nearly cooked through. Add the vegetables and cook for 2 minutes or until tender-crisp. Pour boiling water over the udon noodles to loosen and soften, then drain and add to the pan. Simmer another minute or until the noodles are soft.

Pork Balls with Noodles

Thai-Cured Lamb and Noodle Salad

Serves 4

295 calories per serving; **7.5 g** total fat; **2.7 g** saturated fat; **175 mg** sodium

Thai salads are all the rage, and when looking at a typical list of ingredients, it's hardly surprising. Fragrant inclusions, such as fresh cilantro, mint, lemongrass, and kaffir lime leaves, make the flavor indescribably exotic and almost ethereal. With a dressing of strong lime juice, pungent fish sauce, and often chiles, the lightness of flavor is matched by the lack of calories. Oil is never found in a true Thai dressing.

1 pound lean lamb loin, trimmed

Thai curry paste

2 stalks fresh cilantro with roots

2 tablespoons chopped lemongrass (white part only)

2 tablespoons grated ginger

2 teaspoons chopped lime rind

2 teaspoons brown or palm sugar

1 clove garlic, crushed

Noodle Salad

4 ounces vermicelli or cellophane noodles

2 bird's eye or small red chiles, finely chopped

2 tablespoons finely chopped peanuts (optional)

Dressing

juice of ½ lime

1 teaspoon fish sauce

2 teaspoons reduced-sodium soy sauce

To make the Thai curry paste: Wash and remove the leaves from the cilantro stalks and set aside for the salad. Chop the white root and crush together with the remaining paste ingredients in a mortar and pestle, or briefly in a food processor. Spread over the lamb fillet, cover, and refrigerate overnight.

Soak the noodles in cold water for 10 minutes, drain well then plunge into boiling water for 1 minute or until softened and tender. Drain and toss with the reserved chopped cilantro leaves, chile, and peanuts.

Combine the dressing ingredients.

Heat a heavy-bottomed, nonstick pan to high, brush with oil and sear the lamb for 1–2 minutes each side or as preferred. Don't overcook, or it won't be as tender. Cover loosely with foil and allow to rest for 10 minutes before slicing thinly and serving tossed with the noodle salad. Spoon over the dressing.

Sage and Mint Lamb on Pea Mash

Serves 4

225 calories per serving; **10 g** total fat; **2.8 g** saturated fat; **65 mg** sodium

Serve with salad and crusty bread.

1 potato, peeled and chopped

2 cups frozen or fresh peas

2 teaspoons mint sauce or wine vinegar

8 lean lamb cutlets or leg chops

1 tablespoon olive oil

2 tablespoons fresh chopped sage, or
  1 tablespoon dried

¼ cup white wine

2 tablespoons chopped mint

Boil the potato until nearly cooked, add the peas, and cook until tender. Mash with the mint sauce and keep warm.

Meanwhile, trim any excess fat and sinew from lamb. Brush with the oil and press sage into surface. Heat a large nonstick pan over medium-high heat, add lamb and cook for 4–5 minutes on each side or until nearly cooked. Add the wine and mint and cook for 2 minutes. Serve with the pea mash.

Maple Syrup and Apple Braised Pork with Horseradish Mash

Serves 4

435 calories per serving; **9.5 g** total fat; **2.2 g** saturated fat; **305 mg** sodium

Serve with steamed zucchini and squash.

4 (4-ounce) butterflied pork neck fillets

2 tablespoons dijon mustard

1 tablespoon olive oil

1 cup apple juice

⅓ cup maple syrup

1 tablespoon lemon juice

1 large green apple, peeled, cut into
  quarters, and thinly sliced

3 large potatoes, peeled and chopped

¼ cup well-shaken buttermilk or low-fat milk

1 tablespoon horseradish

freshly ground pepper

Brush the pork fillets with dijon mustard. Heat the oil in a large heavy-bottomed pan and sauté the fillets on high heat for 2 minutes on each side or until browned and crisp. Combine the apple juice, maple syrup, and lemon juice and add to pan. Reduce heat, cover, and simmer over low heat for 25–30 minutes or until pork is tender, turning occasionally and spooning over sauce. Add the apple for the last 10 minutes of cooking time.

Meanwhile, boil the potatoes until tender then mash with the milk, horseradish, and pepper to taste. Keep warm. Remove the pork from the pan, cover with foil, and keep warm. Boil the remaining liquid until thick and syrupy. Serve the pork on the mash and spoon over the sauce.

Pear and Parmesan Risotto with Shaved Pepper Beef

Serves 4

555 calories per serving; **12 g** total fat; **3.8 g** saturated fat; **195 mg** sodium

Try serving this risotto drizzled with a little balsamic vinegar and a mixed green salad. Risottos are so versatile that you can almost always find suitable ingredients in your fridge or pantry to cook one on the spur of the moment. The rice itself is important, and although there are substitutes such as barley and rice-shaped pasta, called orzo, the most common rice for a successful risotto is arborio, originally grown in the Po valley in Italy.

1 tablespoon extra virgin olive oil
1 large firm green pear, peeled and diced
juice and zest of ½ lemon
freshly ground pepper
1 onion, chopped
1½ cups arborio rice
1 cup dry white wine
4 cups hot chicken stock
2–3 leaves fresh basil
2 tablespoons shaved parmesan cheese

Pepper Beef
1 (13-ounce) lean beef fillet
1 tablespoon freshly ground pepper

Heat half the oil in a large heavy-bottomed saucepan. Add the pear and cook for 1–2 minutes or until it starts to soften. Remove from pan, toss in some of the lemon juice, season with pepper, and set aside. Heat the remaining oil and sauté the onion for 1–2 minutes or until translucent. Add rice and cook 1–2 minutes. Pour in wine and cook, stirring until all liquid is absorbed. Add the chicken stock gradually, a ladle or so at a time, and cook, stirring occasionally. After 15 minutes add the pear, then continue adding the stock until rice is cooked, about 5–6 more minutes. Add the remaining lemon juice, zest, and basil. Remove from heat, cover, and allow to sit for 2–3 minutes.

While the rice is cooking, brush the beef with oil, coat with the pepper, and pan-sear on high heat until cooked medium rare or to taste. Remove from pan, cover with foil, and allow to sit for 5–10 minutes before slicing thinly.

To serve, toss the parmesan through the risotto and top with the warm beef.

Roast Lamb Souvlaki

Makes 4 souvlaki

470 calories per serving; **9.5 g** total fat; **2.4 g** saturated fat; **805 mg** sodium

Goat's milk yogurt
is delicious with
this dish.

2 cloves garlic, crushed

grated rind and juice of 1 lemon

12 ounces lamb fillets

2 teaspoons olive oil

4 large pita breads

1 cup shredded butter lettuce

Salad

½ cup chopped parsley

2 tablespoons chopped mint

2 roma tomatoes, diced

½ cucumber, finely diced

2 tablespoons chopped black olives

½ red onion, sliced

Dressing

2 tablespoons low-fat yogurt (see note)

1 clove garlic, crushed

Preheat the oven to 400°F.

Combine the garlic and lemon rind. Brush the lamb with the oil and a little of the lemon juice. Make 5–6 small slits in the top of each fillet. Fill with the garlic lemon mixture. Season to taste with ground pepper. Place on a baking sheet and bake for 12–15 minutes or until medium rare or as preferred. Keep warm, loosely covered with foil.

Combine the salad ingredients. Mix the yogurt with the garlic and remaining lemon juice. Warm the pita breads in a nonstick pan for 30 seconds on each side, top with the lettuce then the salad. Slice the lamb and place on the salad then drizzle with the dressing. Wrap tightly and eat while still warm.

Grilled Steak with Oyster Ragout

Serves 4

235 calories per serving; **8.5 g** total fat; **3 g** saturated fat; **140 mg** sodium

Serve with toasted
Italian bread,
mashed potatoes,
green vegetables,
or salad.

2 teaspoons olive oil

½ leek, white part washed and thinly sliced

2 roma tomatoes, seeded and diced

¼ cup chopped fresh basil

freshly ground pepper

1 tablespoon lemon juice

⅓ cup red wine or beef stock

8 oysters

4 (4-ounce) fillets or lean beef steak (try New York, scotch, or oyster blade fillets)

Heat the oil in a saucepan and cook the leek over low heat until soft. Add the tomato, basil, and pepper to taste and cook for 5 minutes. Add the lemon juice and wine and bring to a boil, then reduce heat to low while steak is cooking. Add the oysters 1–2 minutes before serving to heat through.

Meanwhile, broil or barbecue steak until cooked as desired. Serve with the ragout.

Wine-Braised Veal Shanks with White Bean Purée

Serves 4

410 calories per serving; **11 g** total fat; **1.7 g** saturated fat; **485 mg** sodium

Veal shanks vary greatly in size. However, the gelatinous meat is very satisfying and the most common size available provides enough meat for two people, so choose accordingly.

White bean purée is a natural with veal cooked in this manner, and you can choose from different varieties, such as cannellini, great northern, or lima beans. Always drain and rinse canned beans well before use.

4 small veal shanks, french trimmed
flour, for dusting
2 tablespoons olive oil
1 onion, diced
2 carrots, diced
2 stalks celery, diced
2 cups halved button mushrooms
1 sprig thyme
1 sprig oregano or 2 teaspoons dried
12-ounce can crushed tomatoes
1 cup degreased chicken stock
1 cup white wine
½ cup water

White Bean Purée

1 large potato, peeled and diced
12-ounce can white beans, drained
¼ cup low-fat milk or chicken stock
1 tablespoon finely chopped cilantro
ground black pepper

Trim and discard any fat from the veal. Toss shanks with the flour to coat. Heat 1 tablespoon of the oil in a heavy-bottomed large saucepan and brown the shanks on all sides. Remove from pan, add the remaining oil, onion, carrot, celery, and mushrooms and cook for 2–3 minutes or until onion is soft. Return the veal to the pan with the herbs, tomato, stock, wine, and water. Cover and cook on very low heat for 1½–2 hours or until veal is tender and falls off the bone. Add more water during cooking if needed. When shanks are cooked, skim the top of the liquid well to remove any fat.

When shanks are nearly cooked, place the potato in boiling water and cook for 10 minutes. Add the beans and cook until the vegetables are tender. Drain and purée in a food processor with enough milk or stock to bring to desired consistency. Return to the pan, stir in the cilantro, and season to taste with pepper. Reheat and serve hot with the veal.

Lamb and Eggplant Kebabs with Fattoush

Serves 4

410 calories per serving; **16 g** total fat; **3.8 g** saturated fat; **320 mg** sodium

When cooking kebabs always make sure you soak wooden or bamboo skewers for 30 minutes in cold water before adding the meat and/or other ingredients, or your skewers may burn before the meat is cooked. Metal skewers are always at the ready and cannot burn. They do get very hot though!

Fattoush is a Middle Eastern bread salad, closely related to Italian panzanella. The main difference is in the bread used: pita for fattoush, ciabatta for panzanella.

1 (1-pound) boned leg of lamb or fillet, trimmed of fat
1 clove garlic, crushed
juice and zest of ½ lemon
1 tablespoon olive oil
2 tablespoons yogurt
1 tablespoon chopped fresh parsley
1 large eggplant, cut into large cubes

Fattoush

1 large or 2 small pita breads
1 large cucumber, cubed
3 vine-ripened tomatoes, diced
1 green onion, chopped
½ green bell pepper, diced
½ cup chopped parsley
2 tablespoons lemon juice
1 tablespoon olive oil
1 clove garlic, crushed

Cucumber Raita

(see recipe page 108)

Cut the lamb into bite-sized chunks and place in a large bowl or dish. Combine the garlic, lemon juice and zest, oil, yogurt, and parsley and mix with the lamb. Cover and refrigerate at least 2 hours, or overnight.

To make the fattoush, toast the pita bread in a moderate oven or under a broiler until golden brown and crisp. Crumble into bite-sized pieces and set aside. Toss together the cucumber, tomatoes, green onion, bell pepper, and parsley. Combine the juice, oil, and garlic and toss with the salad. Just before serving stir in the crumbled pita bread.

Thread lamb onto metal or pre-soaked wooden skewers alternately with the eggplant. Broil or barbecue over high heat until cooked as desired. Serve over the fattoush with the Cucumber Raita and lemon wedges.

Peppercorn Beef with Port and Mushroom Sauce

Serves 4

255 calories per serving; **10 g** total fat; **3 g** saturated fat; **110 mg** sodium

Serve with baby potatoes and steamed greens.

4 lean steaks (try short loin, tenderloin, or sirloin)
1 tablespoon olive oil
1 tablespoon crushed peppercorns

Port and Mushroom Sauce

1½ cups sliced shitake or swiss brown mushrooms (or your choice of mushrooms)
1 tablespoon pepper-seasoned flour
1 brown shallot, finely chopped, or
    1 tablespoon finely chopped white onion
¾ cup beef stock
2 teaspoons no-added-salt tomato paste
1 teaspoon reduced-sodium Worcestershire sauce
⅓ cup port or fortified wine
1 tablespoon red wine or cider vinegar

To make the sauce, toss the mushrooms and flour together in a plastic bag and set aside. Cook the shallot in 2 tablespoons of the stock until soft then stir in the tomato paste and sauce. Cook for 1–2 minutes then add the port. Boil for 3 minutes or until it thickens. Add the remaining stock and vinegar and bring to a boil. Add the mushrooms and cook, stirring until mushrooms are soft and mixture is sauce consistency. Keep warm.

Brush steaks with oil and roll in pepper. Barbecue, or broil for 2–3 minutes each side or as preferred. Serve with the mushroom sauce.

Stir-Fried Pork and Sesame Rice

Serves 4

420 calories per serving; **12 g** total fat; **2.1 g** saturated fat; **250 mg** sodium

To curl green onions, soak the green part in iced water for 5 minutes and serve scattered on top as a garnish.

1 (12-ounce) lean pork fillet
1 tablespoon peanut oil
few drops sesame oil
1 tablespoon grated ginger
2 green onions, cut into long diagonal strips
1 red bell pepper, cut into thin strips
1 green bell pepper, cut into thin strips
fresh cilantro leaves

Sauce

1 tablespoon reduced-sodium soy sauce
2 tablespoons rice wine or sherry
2 tablespoons chicken stock
1 tablespoon no-added-salt tomato paste

Sesame Rice

3 cups hot steamed rice
2 tablespoons toasted sesame seeds
few drops sesame oil
2 tablespoons sliced pickled ginger (optional)

Trim any fat from the pork and cut pork into thin pieces. Heat the oils in a wok or large nonstick frying pan and stir-fry the ginger and green onions for 1 minute. Add pork and stir-fry until browned. Add the bell peppers and stir-fry for 1–2 minutes or until they just start to soften.

Combine the sauce ingredients and toss into the pan. Stir a few times to distribute sauce, then reduce heat, cover, and allow to steam for 3–4 minutes. Serve over the hot sesame rice and scatter with cilantro leaves.

To make rice, combine ingredients and toss lightly with a fork.

Lemon and Cheese-Crusted Roast Lamb Loin

Serves 8

225 calories per serving; **9.5 g** total fat; **3 g** saturated fat; **275 mg** sodium

Steamed green beans, snap peas, or asparagus, and grilled tomato are delicious with this dish, as well as a splash of balsamic vinegar over the lamb.

2 pounds boned lamb loins or boned leg of lamb, butterflied

2 tablespoons olive oil

2 tablespoons fresh rosemary leaves

2 tablespoons fresh thyme leaves

juice and coarsely grated rind of 1 lemon

½ cup loosely packed crumbled reduced-fat feta cheese

½ cup coarse fresh bread crumbs

¼ cup fresh chopped parsely

freshly ground pepper

1 tablespoon dijon mustard

Preheat oven to 350°F.

Trim excess fat and sinew off lamb and pound lamb to flatten slightly between sheets of parchment paper. Lay, with the rough interior side facing up, on a work surface. In a food processor, combine 1 tablespoon of the oil with the rosemary, thyme, half the lemon juice, and the lemon rind. Process into a coarse paste. Reserve 1–2 tablespoons of the mixture and combine the remainder with the remaining lemon juice, the cheese, bread crumbs, and parsley, and mix well. Set aside.

Spread the reserved 2 tablespoons of herb mixture over the rough surface of the lamb, leaving a 1-inch border around the edges. Roll lamb up and tie securely with string at regular intervals. Rub remaining oil over surfaces and season with freshly ground pepper. Heat a deep baking dish or nonstick frying pan over high heat and brown the lamb on all sides. Transfer to a wire rack inside the baking dish and roast for 30 minutes.

Transfer the lamb to a cutting board and carefully remove string. Brush with mustard and carefully press cheese mixture onto the top and sides of lamb, pressing firmly to hold in place. Return to the oven and bake for 15 minutes for medium rare. Remove from oven, cover loosely with foil, and leave in a warm place for 10 minutes. Carve into thick slices and serve with vegetables.

Flash-Seared Teriyaki Beef on Glazed Soba Noodles

Serves 4

490 calories per serving; **19 g** total fat; **4 g** saturated fat; **520 mg** sodium

This is delicious with a big cup of miso soup.

1 (1-pound) lean beef tenderloin or fillet

Marinade

2 tablespoons reduced-sodium soy sauce

¼ cup mirin (rice wine) or dry sherry

1 tablespoon rice vinegar

1 tablespoon brown sugar

2 teaspoons grated ginger

Salad

8 ounces soba noodles

1 tablespoon rice wine vinegar

2 tablespoons olive oil

few drops sesame oil

1 tablespoon reduced-sodium soy sauce

2 teaspoons lime or lemon juice

1 tablespoon sesame seeds

2 tablespoons thinly sliced pickled ginger

1 green onion, finely chopped

1 red bell pepper, cut into thin strips

2 stalks crisp celery, thinly sliced

Chill the beef in the freezer until firm, then slice horizontally into thin slices. Combine the marinade ingredients and pour over the beef. Cover and refrigerate for 1 hour. Alternatively, you can marinate the whole fillet, sear the outside quickly, then slice thinly.

Cook the noodles according to directions on the package, then plunge into iced water to cool. Drain well. Whisk together the vinegar, oils, soy sauce, and juice. Toast the sesame seeds in a pan until brown and add the dressing. Place the noodles in a bowl and toss with the dressing and vegetables.

Remove meat from marinade and pat dry. Heat a nonstick frying pan to very hot, brush with oil, add the meat, and sear for 10–20 seconds on each side, brushing continually with marinade. Serve immediately on the noodle salad.

Slow-Roast Beef in Red Wine with Potato Gnocchi

Serves 6

525 calories per serving; **7.5 g** total fat; **1.9 g** saturated fat; **585 mg** sodium

A salad and bread for scooping up the leftovers are ideal accompaniments to this dish.

1 (1½-pound) lean round or sirloin steak, trimmed

¼ cup plain flour

2 teaspoons dried thyme or oregano

freshly ground pepper

2 carrots, sliced

1 parsnip, sliced

2 cups mushrooms, quartered

1 onion, sliced

1 cup red wine

1 cup beef or chicken stock

½ cup water

potato gnocchi (see note)

About gnocchi

Always check the label on gnocchi packets. Avoid the ones with high-fat cheeses, butter, and cream near the start of the ingredients. A bit of butter and parmesan right at the end of the list is all right, but the best gnocchi is straight potato, flour, eggs, and seasonings.

Preheat oven to 325°F.

Cut the meat into large cubes, removing excess fat. Place in a plastic bag with the flour, thyme, and pepper and shake well to coat meat. Place in a large casserole with the vegetables and combine. Pour over the wine, stock, and water and bake for 2½–3 hours or until meat is tender. Halfway through cooking, give the casserole a stir to circulate ingredients. Bring a large pot of water to a boil, add gnocchi, and cook until they rise to the surface—about 10 minutes, or according to instructions. Serve the beef and vegetables over the gnocchi in warmed large bowls to hold the juices.

Soy and Ginger Braised Chicken (page 78)

poultry

Soy and Ginger Braised Chicken

Serves 4

425 calories per serving; **10 g** total fat; **1.9 g** saturated fat; **550 mg** sodium

Snow peas, baby corn, carrots, and broccoli are good vegetables to use.

1 (2-pound) small chicken cut into quarters
1 tablespoon peanut or olive oil
1 tablespoon grated ginger
¾ cup chicken stock
¼ cup sherry
2 tablespoons reduced-sodium soy sauce
1 tablespoon lemon juice
1 tablespoon honey or brown sugar
3 cups mixed Asian vegetables, cut into strips (see note)
2 cups hot steamed rice

Remove all the skin and fat from chicken.

Heat the oil in a heavy-bottomed frying pan, add the ginger, and cook for 1–2 minutes. Add the chicken and brown all over. Turn the chicken flesh side up and pour in the stock, sherry, soy sauce, lemon juice, and honey. Cover tightly, reduce heat, and braise for 45–50 minutes or until very tender and cooked through. Spoon over liquid during cooking to keep the flesh moist. Remove chicken and keep warm. Skim any fat from the surface of the liquid and boil for 5–6 minutes to thin sauce consistency.

In a separate wok or pan, stir-fry the vegetables until tender but still crisp.

To serve, you can either leave the chicken on the bone, or remove and shred the flesh. Serve on the rice with some of the sauce spooned over and the vegetables on the side.

Chinese Chicken Noodle Pancakes

Makes 4 pancakes

295 calories per serving; **9 g** total fat; **2.3 g** saturated fat; **325 mg** sodium

2-ounce package fine noodles such as vermicelli or cellophane
3 eggs
¼ cup plain flour
1 (6½-ounce) cooked chicken breast, cut into thin slivers
½ cup corn kernels
¼ cup snipped chives or green onions
¼ cup chopped fresh cilantro
2 teaspoons reduced-sodium soy or oyster sauce
peanut or olive oil for brushing pan
Glaze
2 tablespoons plum sauce
2 teaspoons reduced-sodium soy sauce
¼ cup sherry or rice wine

Combine the glaze ingredients in a small saucepan and bring to a boil. Reduce heat and keep warm.

Soak the noodles in boiling water for 5 minutes or until soft, drain well, cool, and chop into small pieces. In a large bowl, beat the eggs then fold in the flour, followed by the noodles, chicken, corn, herbs, and soy sauce.

Heat a nonstick pan to high and brush with oil. Pour in ¼ of the mixture and cook until browned underneath and set on top. Turn and brush with the glaze. Cook until browned underneath. Transfer to a plate and keep warm in a low oven while remainder are cooked. Serve hot with leftover glaze spooned over.

Chinese Chicken Noodle Pancakes

Olive, Basil, and Cheese-Filled Chicken Breast

Serves 4

345 calories per serving; **15 g** total fat; **4.1 g** saturated fat; **345 mg** sodium

Serve with crusty Italian or sourdough bread.

To pit olives, simply place them on a wooden board, place a broad knife, such as a cook's knife or a cleaver on top, and press with the flat of your hand. This will split the olive and you can remove the pit. No fancy equipment needed! Pitted olives are available in jars, but the convenience does not make up for the loss of flavor. Olives are best bought in Middle Eastern or Italian delis, where you can sample the many different varieties before buying.

4 (5-ounce) chicken breast fillets
¼ cup pitted black olives
2 teaspoons olive oil
juice of 1 lemon
1 clove garlic, crushed (optional)
freshly ground pepper
8 large leaves basil
2 balls mozzarella, sliced
1 cup dry white wine
1 bunch arugula
4 roma or vine-ripened tomatoes, thickly sliced

Dressing

2 tablespoons balsamic vinegar
1 tablespoon olive oil

Preheat oven to 350°F.

Flatten the chicken breasts between two sheets of parchment paper, or ask your butcher to flatten them for you. Combine the olives, olive oil, 2 teaspoons of the lemon juice, and garlic in a food processor until coarsely ground. You could also finely chop the olives and mash with the oil and lemon, if preferred. Season to taste with pepper.

Lay chicken breasts on a board with the inside facing up and spread with the olive paste. Lay 2 leaves of basil down one side of each breast and top with slices of mozzarella, leaving a border at each end. Tuck in the ends and roll up. Secure with skewers or tie with string and place side-by-side in a casserole dish. Pour in the wine and remaining lemon juice. Some extra basil or cilantro leaves will add to the flavor.

Cover loosely with foil and bake for 30 minutes or until just cooked and the juices run clear when pierced with a knife. Remove foil, brush with a little olive oil, and return to the oven for 5 minutes to crisp the surface. Remove from casserole dish, cover, and allow to sit for 5 minutes.

Arrange the arugula leaves and tomatoes on plates and drizzle with the dressing. Slice each breast in 3–4 large slices and arrange over the salad.

Marinated Chicken and Mung Bean Salad

Serves 4

270 calories per serving; **9 g** total fat; **1.8 g** saturated fat; **330 mg** sodium

Serve this cold or as a hot salad, the choice is yours.

1 pound chicken breast or thigh fillets, cut into strips
1 teaspoon sesame oil
2 tablespoons hoisin sauce
¼ cup sherry or red wine
1 tablespoon grated ginger
1 tablespoon sesame seeds
2 teaspoons peanut or olive oil

Salad

1 cup mung bean or bean sprouts
1 cup shredded red cabbage
1 red bell pepper, thinly sliced
12 snow peas, blanched and cut into strips
2 tablespoons rice wine vinegar
1 teaspoon fish sauce (optional)

Combine the chicken, sesame oil, hoisin, sherry, ginger, and sesame seeds and marinate in the refrigerator at least 2 hours or overnight. Heat a wok or nonstick pan to high and add the peanut oil. When hot, add the chicken and stir-fry for 4–5 minutes or until cooked. Transfer to a shallow pan and chill.

Combine the salad ingredients and toss with the combined vinegar and fish sauce. Serve the chicken scattered over the salad, with a bowl of rice or noodles on the side.

Balsamic-Marinated Chicken with Lemon Couscous

Serves 4

330 calories per serving; **5.5 g** total fat; **1.6 g** saturated fat; **120 mg** sodium

4 (5-ounce) chicken breasts fillets, flattened
¼ cup balsamic vinegar
¼ cup apple juice
1 red bell pepper, roasted, seeded, and peeled
freshly ground pepper

Lemon Couscous

2 cups chicken stock
1 cup couscous
1 tablespoon chopped fresh cilantro
1 tablespoon chopped fresh Italian parsley
1 green onion, thinly sliced
grated zest and juice of 1 lemon
1 teaspoon olive oil

Trim the chicken fillets and place in a deep-sided ceramic dish. Pour over the balsamic vinegar and 2 tablespoons of the apple juice, cover, refrigerate, and marinate overnight. Purée the pepper in a food processor or blender with the remaining apple juice and a little wine or stock if too dry. Season to taste with pepper and set aside.

To make the Lemon Couscous, bring the stock to a boil, add the couscous, herbs, and onion, cover and turn the heat off. Allow to steam for 10 minutes or until all liquid is absorbed. Fluff with a fork, while adding the zest, juice, and oil, and season to taste with pepper. Keep warm.

Drain the marinade from the chicken and broil or barbecue until cooked through, brushing with the marinade during cooking. Serve over the couscous with a spoon of the red pepper purée.

Lemon Turkey Burgers with Herb Mayonnaise

Makes 4 large burgers (Note: high in salt, reduce the amount of Worcestershire sauce, if desired)

475 calories per serving; **11 g** total fat; **2.5 g** saturated fat; **1215 mg** sodium

If you can't buy ground turkey, simply buy fillets, remove the skin and chop finely before putting in the food processor. Or use chicken instead.

Gathering the herbs for a herb mayonnaise can be as easy as stepping out of your kitchen door or snipping away on your window sill. Planted in a sunny position, herbs will flourish even through the winter and whether you have acres of soil or just a few pots on a balcony, the delights of homegrown fresh produce can be yours to reap.

1 small onion, finely chopped
1 pound lean ground turkey (see note)
2 teaspoons grated lemon rind
1 teaspoon thyme leaves
½ cup fresh grated bread crumbs
1 tablespoon reduced-sodium
  Worcestershire sauce
olive oil and lemon juice for brushing burgers
4 thick gourmet buns, such as rye, sourdough,
  grain, or thickly sliced bread
curly lettuce leaves
1 tomato, thickly sliced
1cucumber, thickly sliced

Herb Mayonnaise
¼ cup each chopped parsley and
  cilantro, or mint
1 tablespoon chopped dill
1 green onion, chopped
1 tablespoon low-fat mayonnaise
¼ cup low-fat natural yogurt
2 teaspoons lemon juice
cracked pepper

To make the Herb Mayonnaise, place the fresh herbs and green onion in a food processor or pass through a mill to make a coarse paste. Place in a small bowl with the mayonnaise, yogurt, lemon juice, and pepper and mix well. Cover and chill at least 10 minutes to allow flavors to develop.

Combine onion, turkey, rind, thyme, bread crumbs, and Worcestershire sauce in a food processor and process until well mixed, or mix with hands in a large bowl. Shape into four burgers and barbecue or broil for 5–6 minutes on each side, or until cooked through and no longer pink inside. Brush with olive oil and lemon juice during cooking.

Split bread in half and place on grill at end of cooking to warm. Arrange curly lettuce leaves, thickly sliced tomato and cucumber on bottom half of roll, top with turkey burgers, and a spoonful of the herb mayonnaise.

Warm Chicken and Apple Salad

Serves 6

260 calories per serving; **11 g** total fat; **1.4 g** saturated fat; **130 mg** sodium

This salad is great served with a baguette or rye bread.

½ cup raisins

2 tablespoons port or red wine

½ cup apple juice

¾ pound skinless chicken, diced

2 green apples, diced

2 teaspoons each grated lemon rind and juice

2 stalks celery, chopped

½ cup walnut halves, roasted

1 bunch romaine or mixed lettuce

Dressing

2 tablespoons low-fat natural yogurt

2 tablespoons low-fat mayonnaise

Place the raisins, port, and apple juice in a large saucepan and bring to a boil. Reduce heat, add the chicken, cover, and simmer for 10–15 minutes or until chicken is cooked. Drain and discard liquid.

Place the apples, lemon rind and juice, celery, and walnuts in a bowl and toss to combine. Combine the yogurt and mayonnaise and toss with the salad. Arrange lettuce in a bowl or on plates, top with the salad and spoon over the chicken and raisins.

Hot Chicken Caesar Baguettes with Avocado Dressing

Serves 2

610 calories per serving; **29 g** total fat; **6.9 g** saturated fat; **840 mg** sodium

1 (6-ounce) chicken breast fillet

3 teaspoons extra virgin olive oil

ground black pepper

2 pieces baguette, about 10 inches each

2 large romaine lettuce leaves

2 hard-boiled free-range eggs, quartered

2 teaspoons shredded parmesan cheese

Dressing

½ avocado, chopped

2 anchovies, drained and rinsed

1 tablespoon low-fat yogurt

1 tablespoon lemon juice

1 teaspoon reduced-sodium Worcestershire sauce

Beat together the dressing ingredients until smooth and set aside.

Brush the chicken with 1 teaspoon of the oil, season to taste with pepper, and broil until cooked through. Split the baguettes in half lengthwise and brush with the remaining oil.

Lay open on a baking sheet and bake or broil until crisp and hot. Place a lettuce leaf on each baguette, top with the chicken and egg, and spoon over some dressing. Sprinkle with the parmesan, close the baguette, and eat while hot.

Penne with Char-Broiled Chicken and Eggplant

Serves 4

680 calories per serving; **12 g** total fat; **3 g** saturated fat; **275 mg** sodium

When choosing pasta to match a hearty, chunky sauce, select short, chunky shapes, such as penne, rigatoni, pipe, conchiglie, casareccia, gnocchi, fusilli, elicoidali, and maccheroni. When choosing pasta to match a thin, creamy, clingy sauce, select long shapes, such as spaghetti, spaghettini, vermicelli, capellini, fedelini, linguine, fettuccine, trenette, and tagliolini.

1 pound penne pasta

1 tablespoon extra virgin olive oil

1 pound chicken breast or thigh fillets

4 thick slices eggplant

1 clove garlic, crushed

2 green onions, sliced

2 tablespoons semi-dried tomatoes, sliced

2 roma tomatoes, seeded and diced

2 teaspoons fresh oregano leaves

¼ cup chicken stock

¼ cup dry white wine

2 cups sliced arugula or baby spinach leaves

¼ cup reduced-fat feta cheese, rinsed and crumbled

Cook the pasta according to directions, drain well, toss with a teaspoon of the oil, and keep warm. Brush the chicken and eggplant with oil and season to taste with pepper. Char-broil both in a preheated broiling pan or heavy-bottomed frying pan for 1–2 minutes on each side or until the chicken is browned but not cooked right through and the eggplant is brown and soft. Remove from pan and set aside.

Heat the remaining oil in a large frying pan and sauté the garlic and green onions for 1–2 minutes or until soft. Add both the tomatoes and oregano and cook for 2–3 minutes. Add the stock and wine and bring to a boil. Slice the chicken thickly and add to the pan.

Cover, reduce the heat, and cook for 5–6 minutes or until chicken is cooked. Add the arugula and cook for 1 minute, then toss with the pasta, and heat through. Serve topped with the crumbled feta.

Turkey and Garden Vegetable Terrine with Oregano and Thyme

Serves 6

190 calories per serving; **10 g** total fat; **1.9 g** saturated fat; **240 mg** sodium

Serve cold or reheated, with salad and bread, or sliced on a sandwich.

Turkey meat is a good source of iron and protein and is low in fat.

Terrine is not only the name of the finished dish but also the vessel it is cooked in, originally an earthenware, ovenproof dish.

1–2 tablespoons white wine

2 green onions, chopped

1 cup sliced mushrooms

1 pound ground turkey or chicken breast (or finely chopped skinless breast and thigh meat)

1 egg

½ cup low-fat milk

1 tablespoon fresh oregano leaves or 1 teaspoon dried

1 tablespoon fresh thyme leaves or 1 teaspoon dried

2 tablespoons chopped fresh parsley or basil

freshly ground pepper

1 carrot, diced

1 zucchini, diced

½ cup chopped pistachio nuts

3–4 large spinach or large butter lettuce leaves, lightly blanched

Preheat oven to 350ºF. Line a 9 by 5-inch loaf pan with plastic wrap, leaving an overhang to cover the top of the terrine.

Heat the wine and cook the onions and mushrooms until soft. Cool. Place the turkey and egg in a food processor and process to a fine paste. Add the milk and herbs, season with pepper, and pulse on and off until ingredients are just incorporated. Cover and refrigerate. Lightly blanch or steam the carrot and zucchini until just tender. Drain and pat dry with a paper towel.

Fold all the vegetables and nuts through the mixture. Line the prepared loaf pan with the spinach leaves. Spoon in mixture and press down well. Top with spinach and enclose with plastic over top. Cover with foil. Place in a large deep-sided baking dish and pour in enough boiling water to come ⅔ of the way up the sides. Bake for 1 hour or until juices run clear when tested with a skewer or sharp knife.

Remove foil and plastic from top and cool to room temperature on a wire rack. Unmold on a tray to allow juices to escape. Return to clean loaf pan, cover, and refrigerate overnight.

Chicken, Macadamia Nut, and Noodle Stir-Fry

Serves 4

650 calories per serving; **23 g** total fat; **3.6 g** saturated fat; **630 mg** sodium

These noodles can be found in Asian food stores and most supermarkets.

1 pound skinless, boneless chicken breast, sliced

¼ cup dry sherry or rice wine

2 tablespoons oyster sauce

1 tablespoon reduced-sodium soy sauce

2 teaspoons cornstarch

12-ounce package rice or soba noodles (see note)

½ cup raw whole and half macadamia nuts

1 tablespoon peanut or macadamia nut oil

1 knob ginger, sliced

2 green onions, chopped

1 red bell pepper, sliced

2 cups chopped asparagus or green beans

⅓–½ cup chicken stock

Place chicken in a bowl and mix with the sherry, sauces, and cornstarch. Cover and marinate in the refrigerator for at least 30 minutes. Cover noodles with boiling water and soak 10–15 minutes to soften. Drain.

Heat a wok and stir-fry macadamia nuts until golden. Remove from pan, add half the oil, and stir-fry ginger 1 minute, add vegetables and stir-fry 2 minutes. Set aside. Add remaining oil, remove chicken from marinade, and stir-fry 3–5 minutes or until just cooked. Add vegetables, ⅓ cup of the stock and noodles and toss together until heated through, adding more stock if necessary. Add macadamia nuts just before serving.

Lemon and Almond-Crusted Chicken on Sweet Potato Mash

Serves 4

330 calories per serving; **13 g** total fat; **2.5 g** saturated fat; **150 mg** sodium

Serve with a big green side salad or steamed greens.

1 tablespoon extra virgin olive oil

1 tablespoon lemon juice

4 (4-ounce) chicken breast or thigh fillets

2 tablespoons grated lemon zest

2 tablespoons finely chopped or ground almonds

2 teaspoons grated parmesan cheese

½–1 cup chicken stock

Sweet Potato Mash

1½ cups peeled and diced sweet potato

¼ cup buttermilk or low-fat milk

cracked black pepper

Preheat the oven to 350°F.

Combine the oil and 1 teaspoon of the lemon juice and brush over the chicken fillets. Pan-fry in a nonstick pan for 1–2 minutes each side to brown the surface. Transfer the fillets to an ovenproof dish. Combine the remaining juice, lemon zest, almonds, and parmesan cheese and press over the top of the chicken. Pour in enough chicken stock to come to about ½ inch up the dish. Bake for 30–40 minutes or until cooked through.

Meanwhile, cook the sweet potato until tender, mash, and stir in the buttermilk and pepper to taste. Reheat and serve topped with the chicken.

Satay-Crusted Chicken and Basmati Pilau

Serves 4

515 calories per serving; **11 g** total fat; **2 g** saturated fat; **155 mg** sodium

Check the label on peanut butters. Unnecessary added fats, sugar, and salt often replace the wonderful natural oils and nutrients of the peanuts. Try a freshly ground one from a health food store. Just buy a small amount and keep in the fridge.

Basmati rice is frequently chosen for pilau because of its long grain, giving the dish a fluffy result, while the grains remain separate and firm. Basmati also has a deliciously fragrant flavor.

4 (4-ounce) chicken breast fillets
⅓ cup roasted unsalted peanuts or ¼ cup
  crunchy roasted peanut butter (see note)
1 red chile, chopped or 1 teaspoon chile sauce
2 teaspoons reduced-sodium soy sauce
2 teaspoons lemon juice
1 clove garlic, crushed
lemon wedges and a salad, to serve

Pilau
1 white onion, diced
2 teaspoons olive oil
1½ cups basmati rice
3 cups water
1 bay leaf
1 teaspoon fresh thyme leaves
½ cup chopped green beans
1 tablespoon chopped flat-leaf parsley

Cut each fillet into 3 long strips. In a food processor, combine the peanuts, chile, soy sauce, lemon juice, and garlic. Purée to a coarse paste, so there are still some chunks of nuts. Add a little water if mixture is too coarse. Spread over the chicken, cover, and refrigerate for 1 hour.

In a large saucepan, sauté the onion in the oil until soft. Add the rice and sauté for 1 minute. Add the water, bay leaf, and thyme and bring to a boil. Reduce the heat to low, cover, and simmer for 20 minutes. Add the beans and parsley and cook 5–7 minutes or until rice is tender and liquid is absorbed. If your saucepan doesn't have a very tight seal, you may need to add more water during cooking.

While the rice is cooking, place the chicken in the broiler and cook under a medium heat for 5–6 minutes each side or until cooked through. Serve with the hot rice, lemon wedges, and a salad.

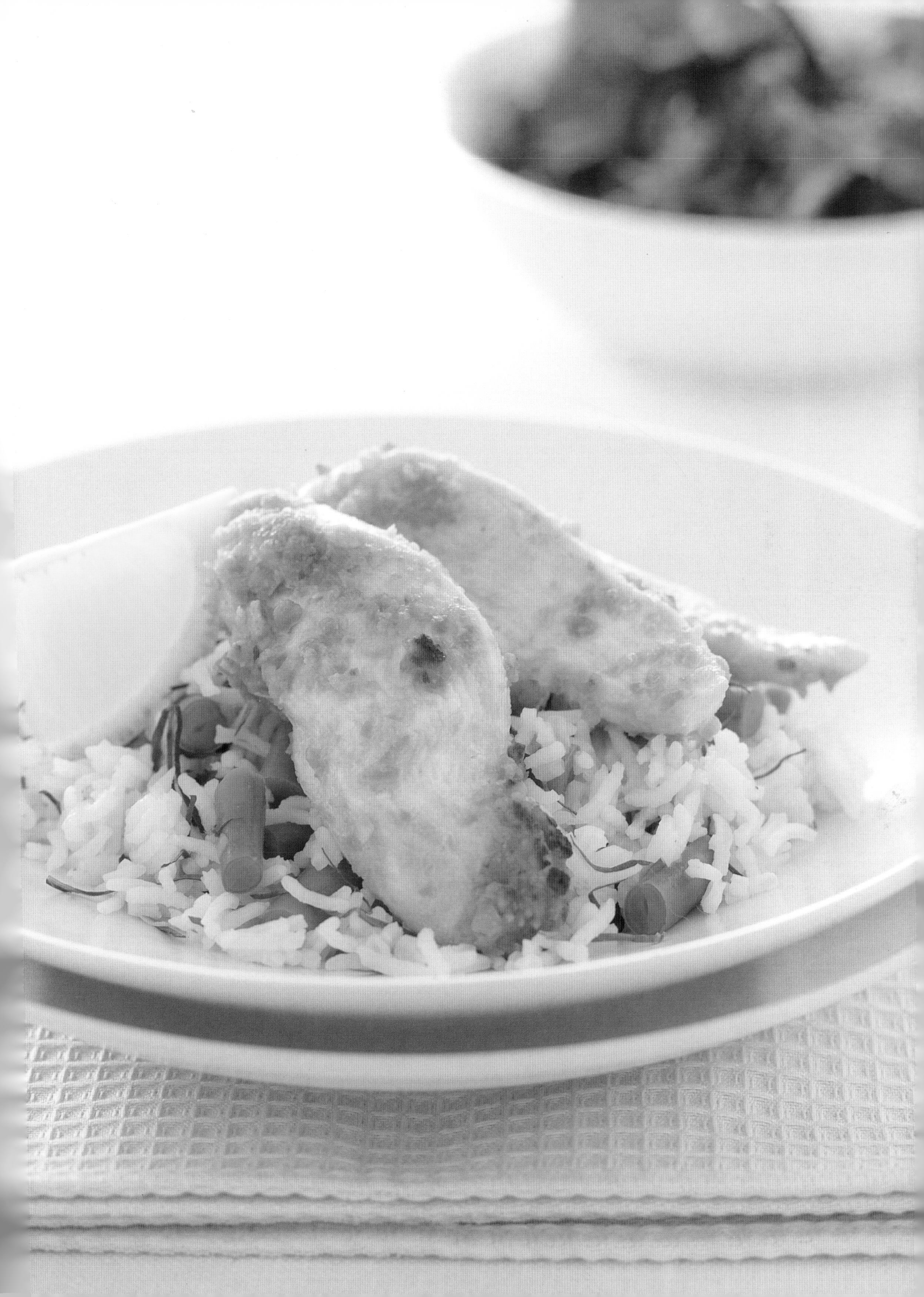

Mediterranean Chicken Strudel

Makes 4 strudels

345 calories per serving; **12 g** total fat; **3.3 g** saturated fat; **360 mg** sodium

Serve as a meal with a large side salad and bread or just enjoy as a snack.

1 large red bell pepper

4 spinach leaves

4 (5-ounce) chicken breast fillets

olive oil and fresh lemon juice, for brushing

⅓ cup fresh low-fat ricotta cheese

2 teaspoons grated lemon rind

freshly ground pepper

8 sheets filo pastry

1 tablespoon grated parmesan cheese

Preheat oven to 350°F.

Cut the bell pepper in quarters, remove seeds, and roast, skin side up until skin blackens. Seal in a bag for 10 minutes, then peel. Blanch or steam the spinach leaves until they just start to soften. Pat dry and set aside.

Flatten chicken breast fillets to about ½ inch thickness or cut fillet horizontally and fold out like a butterfly. Brush with a little olive oil and lemon. Spread ricotta over one side of the fillet and season with lemon rind and pepper. Top with a slice of the roasted red pepper.

Fold one half of the chicken over the other and wrap in a spinach leaf.

Lay 2 sheets of filo pastry on a dry board, brush with oil, and season with pepper. Place chicken parcel on one end, fold in the ends, and wrap up like a parcel. Brush top with oil.

Sprinkle with parmesan and bake on a lightly oiled or lined baking sheet for 25–30 minutes or until chicken is cooked.

Thai Chicken Curry with Papaya Raita

Serves 4

360 calories per serving; **9 g** total fat; **3 g** saturated fat; **180 mg** sodium

Using water makes a lighter, fresher curry. For a creamier, richer texture, use evaporated skim milk.

2 teaspoons extra virgin olive oil

1 clove garlic, crushed

2 spring onions, chopped

1 stalk lemongrass, white part only, chopped

1 tablespoon green curry paste

1 pound chicken breast fillets, sliced

¾ cup water (see note)

½ cup light coconut milk

1 kaffir lime leaf

1 red bell pepper, finely diced

1 cucumber, seeded and diced

2 cups steamed Thai jasmine rice, to serve

Papaya Raita

1 cup finely diced papaya

juice of 1 lime

½ cucumber, grated

¼ cup low-fat yogurt

Heat the oil in a large saucepan. Add the garlic, onion, and lemongrass and cook until soft. Add the curry paste and chicken and cook until chicken is browned. Add the water, coconut milk, and lime leaf and bring to a boil. Cook for 20 minutes then add the pepper and cucumber. Cook for 20 minutes or until chicken is tender and sauce is thick and fragrant.

While the chicken is cooking combine the raita ingredients in a bowl and mix well. Set aside until ready to serve. Remove leaf from curry and serve with rice and the Papaya Raita.

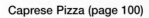
Caprese Pizza (page 100)

no meat

Caprese Pizza

Serves 4

485 calories per serving; **24 g** total fat; **9.6 g** saturated fat; **680 mg** sodium

You can use store-bought, ready-to-bake pizza crust or try using a large loaf of focaccia bread.

1 pizza crust (see note)
2 tablespoons olive oil
1 clove garlic, cut in half
4 roma tomatoes, sliced
16 large fresh leaves basil
4 (2-ounce) mozzarella balls, sliced
cracked black pepper
1 tablespoon capers, rinsed (optional)

Preheat oven to 375°F.

Brush the crust with oil, and rub with the garlic. Arrange tomato, basil, and mozzarella on the bread. Season to taste with pepper and scatter with capers. Bake for 10–15 minutes or until cheese is golden and base is crisp, then place under a broiler for 2 minutes, or until the cheese browns. Serve straight from the oven.

Char-Broiled Vegetable Salad with Dill Cheese Dressing

Serves 4

165 calories per serving; **12 g** total fat; **2.4 g** saturated fat; **130 mg** sodium

Serve with lemon wedges and thickly sliced bread or over a bowl of pasta. It is also nice sitting on a bed of lettuce.

2 tablespoons olive oil
3 tablespoons lime or lemon juice
¼ cup crumbled reduced-fat goat or feta cheese
1 tablespoon dill leaves
2 small zucchini, cut into 3 lengthwise
2 red bell peppers, seeded, halved and pressed flat
2 Belgian endives, halved lengthwise
cracked pepper
8 large flat mushrooms

Heat a broiler or barbecue to high. Combine the oil and lemon juice and purée half in a food processor with the cheese to a smooth paste. Alternatively, mash all together with a fork in a small bowl. Stir in the dill and set aside. Cook the zucchini, red pepper, and endive under the broiler or on the hot grill for 5–6 minutes, turning and brushing with the remaining oil and juice or until tender and slightly browned. Season to taste with pepper.

Add the mushrooms halfway through cooking and grill until juices start to escape. Serve vegetables with a spoonful of the dressing.

Char-Broiled Vegetable Salad with Dill Cheese Dressing

Spicy Noodle and Peanut Sang Choy Bow

Makes 6

150 calories per serving; **4.5 g** total fat; **0.6 g** saturated fat; **150 mg** sodium

6-ounce package hokkien or soba noodles

few drops sesame oil

1 tablespoon reduced-sodium soy sauce

2 teaspoons plum or oyster sauce

¼ cup roasted peanuts, roughly chopped

1 cup bean sprouts

½ cup shredded carrot

1 green onion, chopped

2 tablespoons chopped fresh cilantro

6 firm large lettuce leaves, such as
  radicchio or butter lettuce

Cook the noodles according to directions and drain well. Place in a bowl and toss with the oil and sauces. Add the peanuts, sprouts, carrot, green onion, and cilantro, and toss to combine. Spoon mixture into lettuce cups and serve right away.

Lemon Vegetable Pilaf

Serves 4

495 calories per serving; **12 g** total fat; **1.2 g** saturated fat; **50 mg** sodium

1 tablespoon olive oil

⅓ cup slivered almonds

¼ cup chopped dried apricots

¼ cup sliced dates

1 teaspoon ground cinnamon

1 onion, chopped

1½ cups basmati rice

2 teaspoons ground cumin

pinch saffron

1 teaspoon allspice

1½ cups vegetable stock

½ cup white wine

juice and grated zest of 1 lemon

1 cup cauliflower florets

1 cup broccoli florets

1 cup peas

Heat 2 teaspoons of the oil in a large saucepan. Add the almonds, apricots, dates, and cinnamon and cook, stirring until nuts are golden brown. Remove from the pan, drain on absorbent paper, and set aside.

Add the remaining 2 teaspoons oil and the onion to the pan and cook until onions are soft. Add the rice, cumin, saffron, and allspice to the pan and cook, stirring for 1–2 minutes. Pour in the stock, wine, and lemon and bring to a boil. Reduce heat to low, add the cauliflower, cover with a tight-fitting lid, and cook for 15 minutes.

Add the remaining vegetables and a little more water or stock if mixture is dry. Cover and cook for a further 5–7 minutes or until the rice is cooked and vegetables are tender. Serve scattered with the reserved almond fruit mixture.

Asparagus and Pine Nut Tarts

Makes 6 regular muffin-sized tarts

330 calories per serving; **19 g** total fat; **3.4 g** saturated fat; **80 mg** sodium

Ricotta has a high moisture content and in some cases draining it in a lined colander may be necessary. Best eaten on the day you've bought it, ricotta has a fresh, light flavor and makes a light dessert, with fruit or nuts, or simply drizzled with a little honey, or dusted with cocoa powder.

Pine nuts have a high oil content— 81 percent unsaturated (equally mono and polyunsaturated), good protein and iron, and a sweet flavor. Keep refrigerated, because rancidity can be a problem. Roasting improves the flavor.

Pastry

- ½ cup pine nuts
- 1½ cups flour
- 2 tablespoons olive oil
- ½ cup low-fat milk
- 1 teaspoon grated lemon rind

Filling

- 8–10 spears fresh asparagus
- ¾ cup fresh low-fat ricotta cheese
- ¼ cup low-fat yogurt
- 1–2 tablespoons chopped fresh dill
- cracked pepper
- 2 tablespoons pine nuts, plus extra

To make pastry, place pine nuts in a food processor and process for 30 seconds or until they have started to break up. Add the flour and process until combined. Combine the oil, milk, and lemon rind, and gradually pour in with the motor running until the mixture clumps and forms a dough. Transfer to a well-floured board and knead until smooth. Wrap in plastic and refrigerate for 30 minutes.

Preheat oven to 350°F.

Roll out pastry and cut to fit six muffin or tart pans. Gently ease into lightly oiled pans and prick base evenly with a fork. Bake for 15 minutes then allow to cool for 10 minutes.

Plunge the asparagus into boiling water, cook for 30 seconds then run under cold water to stop cooking. Pat dry with a paper towel and cut into 1-inch lengths. Beat together the ricotta, yogurt, and dill and season to taste with pepper. Spoon mixture into tarts and top with asparagus and pine nuts. Return to the oven and bake for 8–10 minutes or until the filling has set. Serve the tarts hot or cold.

Roasted Fennel, Carrot, and Walnut Salad

Serves 6

160 calories per serving; **12 g** total fat; **1.3 g** saturated fat; **80 mg** sodium

Enjoy with some crusty, hot sourdough or wood-fired bread and fresh ricotta cheese.

2 fennel bulbs

4 carrots

2 tablespoons olive oil

¼ cup walnut halves and pieces

6–8 leaves basil, torn

2 tablespoons red wine vinegar

1 tablespoon lemon juice

baby spinach, to serve

Preheat oven to 350ºF.

Remove any tough outer stalks and the green leaves from the fennel. Cut each into 6–8 wedges from top to bottom. Peel the carrots and cut each into 4 wedges. Brush the fennel and carrot with 1 tablespoon of the oil and place on an oiled baking sheet or casserole dish. Bake for 30 minutes or until nearly tender. Add the walnuts and basil and cook for 5 minutes or until walnuts are crisp and aromatic.

Whisk the remaining oil, vinegar, and juice together. Serve the roast vegetables and walnuts on a bed of baby spinach leaves. Spoon over the dressing.

Pumpkin and Cannellini Toasted Sandwiches

Makes 4 sandwiches

180 calories per serving; **3 g** total fat; **1 g** saturated fat; **510 mg** sodium

These toasted sandwiches are delicious with a mixture of tomato sauce and yogurt for an easy Sunday night snack.

1 cup grated pumpkin

⅓ cup canned, drained cannellini or white beans

2 tablespoons chopped fresh cilantro

½ teaspoon ground cumin

8 slices bread

2 tablespoons grain mustard

2 tablespoons low-fat fresh ricotta

Combine the pumpkin, beans, cilantro, and cumin in a small bowl and mix well. Spread bread with mustard on one side, ricotta on the other, and place a spoonful of the mixture in the center of each sandwich. Cook in a sandwich maker or just toast under the broiler.

Potato, Chickpea, and Cashew Curry

Serves 6

260 calories per serving; **11 g** total fat; **1.8 g** saturated fat; **275 mg** sodium

When cooking curries, spices are often the most important flavoring. Buy spices whole, never ground—these lose their flavor very quickly once the jar is opened

To roast spices, place them in a dry frying pan and set over moderate heat. Shake the pan from time to time and roast until you can smell their particular aroma, and little wafts of smoke start to escape. This will take only a few minutes. Don't burn them, as they will become bitter. Use a mortar or clean coffee grinder to grind the spices.

1 tablespoon olive oil
1 tablespoon mustard seeds
1 teaspoon coriander seeds
1 teaspoon cumin seeds
1 tablespoon chopped ginger
1 large onion, chopped
1 tablespoon curry paste (mild or hot)
12 ounces potatoes, peeled and diced
12-ounce can chickpeas, drained and
  well rinsed
12-ounce can diced tomatoes, no added salt
½ cup vegetable stock or water
½ cup dry-roasted cashews
1 cup green beans

Cucumber Raita

1 cup natural low-fat yogurt
1 cucumber, grated
2 tablespoons chopped mint
2 tablespoons lemon juice

Heat oil in a large, heavy-bottomed saucepan and cook the mustard, coriander, and cumin seeds until they start to pop. Add the ginger, onion, and curry paste and cook for 2–3 minutes or until onion is soft. Add the potato, chickpeas, tomatoes, and stock and bring to a boil. Reduce heat, cover, and simmer for 20–30 minutes, or until potato is tender, adding more water if necessary. Stir in the cashews.

Meanwhile combine the Cucumber Raita ingredients and refrigerate until ready to serve.

Steam or blanch the beans until just tender. Keep warm.

Serve curry surrounded by the beans and with the Cucumber Raita separately.

Risoni with Roast Vegetables and Almond Pesto

Serves 4

675 calories per serving; **22 g** total fat; **3 g** saturated fat; **50 mg** sodium

A splash of balsamic or red wine vinegar and a grind of pepper give this dish an added lift, and some Italian bread is great for soaking up any leftover pesto.

1 cup diced pumpkin

3 small zucchini, chopped

olive oil, to brush

ground black pepper

herbs of choice

1 large red bell pepper, halved and seeded

1 bunch asparagus, each spear cut
   into 3 even lengths

12 cherry tomatoes, halved

1 pound risoni pasta

Almond Pesto

¼ cup dry-roasted almonds

1 cup chopped fresh basil

½ cup chopped fresh cilantro or parsley

1 tablespoon lemon juice

2 tablespoons extra virgin olive oil

1 tablespoon grated parmesan cheese

Preheat the oven to 350°F.

Place the pumpkin and zucchini on a lined baking sheet, brush with olive oil, and season to taste with pepper or herbs of choice. Roast for 20 minutes or until the pumpkin is tender. Add the red pepper, asparagus, and tomatoes, cut side up, after 10 minutes of cooking. Remove from the oven, allow to cool slightly, then peel the pepper and cut into ½-inch thick slices.

While the vegetables are roasting, cook the risoni according to directions on the package. Drain and keep warm.

Place the pesto ingredients in a food processor and process to a coarse paste, adding a little stock or vinegar if the mixture is too thick for your taste. Toss a tablespoon of the pesto through the hot risoni. Serve topped with the roasted vegetables and remaining pesto.

Spinach, Mushroom, and Tofu Lasagne

Serves 2 as a light meal

280 calories per serving; **22 g** total fat; **3 g** saturated fat; **340 mg** sodium

9-ounce block fresh firm silken tofu

8 oyster mushrooms

1 tablespoon extra virgin olive oil

1 tablespoon rice wine vinegar

1 tablespoon reduced-sodium soy sauce

few drops sesame oil

2 cups baby spinach leaves, cut into
   long thin strips

1 tablespoon sesame seeds, plus
   2 teaspoons extra

Drain tofu well and cover with a paper towel. Place on a plate and refrigerate for 20 minutes. Lightly sauté or broil oyster mushrooms until they just start to soften and lose moisture. Set aside. Whisk together the oil, vinegar, soy sauce, and sesame oil. Slice the block of tofu in half horizontally, then slice each piece in half, so each portion has 2 pieces of tofu.

Just before serving, toast the sesame seeds and toss one tablespoon through the dressing—they should sizzle as the hot hits the cold and the flavors infuse.

To serve, place one slice of tofu on a plate, top with a mushroom then some of the spinach. Repeat, drizzle with the dressing, and sprinkle with the remaining sesame seeds. Serve immediately.

Potato Burgers with Roast Tomato Relish

Makes about 6 burgers

185 calories per serving (without bread rolls); **5.5 g** total fat; **1 g** saturated fat; **40 mg** sodium

The relish can be stored in the refrigerator for a few days in a sealed container, or served hot with the burgers. Serve the burgers on arugula leaves or bread rolls with salad and the relish.

Roasting tomatoes brings out their flavor, particularly during winter, when these—essentially summer—fruits are not at their best. The addition of balsamic vinegar and fresh basil ensure a lively relish, no matter what time of year.

3 large potatoes, peeled and diced
½ cup sliced leek
½ red bell pepper, raw or roasted and chopped
1 teaspoon thyme leaves
2 tablespoons fresh parsley
2 eggs, lightly beaten
pepper-seasoned flour, for coating
1 tablespoon olive oil

Roast tomato relish

6 roma tomatoes, peeled and diced
1 red onion, diced
1 tablespoon brown sugar
2 tablespoons balsamic vinegar
¼ cup chopped fresh basil
cracked pepper

Preheat the oven to 350°F.

To make the relish, toss all ingredients together and place in a lightly-oiled baking dish. Bake for 20 minutes or until onion is soft. Mash with a fork or blend in a food processor. Set aside (see note).

To make the burgers, cook the potatoes until just tender, adding leek about halfway through cooking time. Mash and allow to cool for 10 minutes. Place in a bowl with the red pepper, thyme, parsley, and eggs and mix well. Shape into burgers and coat with flour. Lay on a lined baking sheet and refrigerate for 30 minutes. Heat oil in a nonstick pan and fry cakes for 5 minutes each side or until golden brown. Keep warm in a low oven while remainder are cooked. Serve immediately with the relish.

Tagliatelle with Mixed Mushroom Sauce

Serves 4

540 calories per serving; **6.5 g** total fat; **2 g** saturated fat; **80 mg** sodium

An arugula and parmesan salad is an ideal accompaniment for this dish, with some sliced vine-ripened tomatoes.

¼ cup dried porcini or other dried mushrooms

2 large field mushrooms

10 mushrooms of choice such as shitake, swiss, or oyster mushrooms

2 teaspoons extra virgin olive oil

1 clove garlic, crushed

1 spring onion, sliced

¾ cup white wine

⅓ cup fresh ricotta cheese

1 tablespoon lemon juice

freshly ground pepper

1 pound tagliatelle or fettuccine

2 tablespoons chopped flat-leaf parsley, plus extra fresh parsley or basil, to serve

Cover the dried mushrooms with boiling water and soak for 20 minutes. Drain and reserve a few tablespoons of the liquid. Thickly slice all the mushrooms. Heat the oil in a large high-sided frying pan and sauté the garlic and onion for 1 minute to soften. Add all the mushrooms and cook for 2–3 minutes or until they start to release their juices.

Add a few tablespoons of the wine to the ricotta and juice and mix together until smooth. Add to pan with the remaining wine and simmer until sauce thickens. Check for seasoning, and add pepper or extra lemon juice to taste.

Meanwhile cook the tagliatelle according to directions on the package, strain and toss through the sauce, together with the chopped parsley. Serve sprinkled with fresh parsley or basil.

Ricotta, Pine Nut, and Couscous Frittata

Serves 8

180 calories per serving; **8.5 g** total fat; **2.6 g** saturated fat; **90 mg** sodium

For the simplest way to peel and seed tomatoes, see the note on page 36.

2 teaspoons olive oil

1 red onion, chopped

1 zucchini, thinly sliced

2 roma tomatoes, peeled, seeded (see note) and diced

2 tablespoons currants

2 teaspoons each lemon zest and juice

¼ cup chopped fresh mint

¼ cup chopped fresh parsley

1 cup cooked couscous (see directions on package)

½ cup ricotta cheese

6 eggs

2 tablespoons pine nuts

Preheat the broiler.

Heat the oil in a large nonstick frying pan. Add the onion and zucchini and cook for 2–3 minutes or until soft. Add the tomatoes, currants, zest, herbs, and couscous and cook for 1–2 minutes. Beat the cheese and eggs together in a bowl, then pour over the mixture. Cook over a medium heat until the base is browned and the top is nearly set. Sprinkle with pine nuts and place under the broiler until golden brown. Slice and serve hot or cold with salad.

Barley and Bean Salad

Serves 6

325 calories per serving; **16 g** total fat; **2.4 g** saturated fat; **170 mg** sodium

Serve as a side or main dish over a bed of arugula or mixed lettuce.

Full of goodness, barley is one of the earliest cultivated grains, and is again gaining popularity in the western world. The most commonly used form is pearl barley —the hulled barley grain. Buy barley in healthfood shops with a good turnover and store in a cool, dark place. Barley is also used in soups and pilafs and you can use barley cooking water to make barley water, usually flavored with lemon, lime, or orange.

1 cup barley

12-ounce can navy beans, drained and well rinsed

¼ cup chopped cilantro leaves

2 tomatoes, diced

2 green onions, diced

1 cup corn kernels

1 avocado, diced

½ cup chopped string beans or celery

⅓ cup roasted hazelnuts, roughly chopped

Dressing

1 tablespoon olive or hazelnut oil

2 tablespoons red wine vinegar

1 tablespoon lemon juice

Place the barley in a large pot of boiling water and cook for 30 minutes or until tender but not soft. Drain, refresh under cold running water and allow to cool. In a large bowl combine the barley with the remaining salad ingredients.

To make the dressing, whisk together the oil, vinegar, and juice and toss through the salad.

Peach and Pear Tart (page 12

dessert

Peach and Pear Tart

Makes a 10-inch tart

185 calories per serving; **6.5 g** total fat; **1.8 g** saturated fat; **75 mg** sodium

½ cup ricotta cheese

2 tablespoons custard powder

½ teaspoon vanilla extract

3 canned pears, peeled and diced

3 fresh or canned peaches, drained

apple or pear jelly for glazing

Pastry

¼ cup dry-roasted almonds, chopped

2 tablespoons cornstarch

1¼ cups plain flour

1 teaspoon grated lemon rind

1 tablespoon sugar

2 tablespoons margarine

⅓ cup chilled skim milk

¼ cup cold water

To make pastry, place the almonds, cornstarch, flour, lemon, sugar, and margarine in a food processor and press the pulse button until mixture resembles bread crumbs. With motor running, gradually pour in the milk and then water until mixture starts to clump and form a dough. Turn onto a floured board and knead gently to a smooth dough. Wrap in plastic and refrigerate 30 minutes.

Preheat oven to 375°F. Roll out to fit a flan or pie dish. Gently ease into lightly oiled dish and prick evenly with a fork. Bake for 15–20 minutes or until golden brown. Transfer to a wire rack to cool. This can be made a few days ahead of time and stored in a sealed container until ready to fill.

To make the filling, beat together the ricotta, custard powder, vanilla, and ¼ of a pear. Spoon into tarts and top with fruit. Warm jelly in microwave for 10 seconds or over hot water until just soft and spoon over fruit.

Rum and Ricotta Tiramisu

Serves 8

220 calories per serving; **9.5 g** total fat; **5.7 g** saturated fat; **200 mg** sodium

For a special liqueur touch, add a tablespoon of Kahlua, Baileys Irish Cream, or other coffee liqueur to the coffee.

1 cup low-fat ricotta cheese

¾ cup light cream cheese

1 tablespoon rum or cognac

¼ cup superfine sugar

1½ cups very strong espresso or good quality coffee, cooled

16 ladyfingers

2 tablespoons unsweetened cocoa, for dusting

Beat the cheeses, rum, and sugar with electric beaters until light and creamy, set aside. Pour the coffee into a large shallow dish. Quickly dip one side of half the ladyfingers into the coffee and lay closely together with the dipped side down over the base of a large flat-based serving dish. Spread half of the cheese mixture evenly over the lady-fingers. Dust with half the cocoa then repeat layers with coffee-dipped biscuits and cheese. Cover with plastic wrap and refrigerate for at least 6 hours or overnight. Dust with remaining cocoa just before serving.

Rum and Ricotta Tiramisu

Sauterne Cake with Berries and Crème Anglaise

Makes a 9-inch cake and 1½ cups Crème Anglaise

365 calories per serving; **18 g** total fat; **3.2 g** saturated fat; **50 mg** sodium

This cake is equally at home on the afternoon tea table or as a dessert.

Sauterne, a classic dessert wine, contributes sweetness and ensures a moist texture.

Serve the cake with fresh berries in summer—at other times of the year, try some poached or stewed fruit in season, such as plums, apples, or pears.

3 eggs, separated, plus 1 egg white

½ cup superfine sugar

grated rind of 1 lemon

⅓ cup extra virgin olive oil

⅓ cup sauterne or sweet dessert wine

1¼ cups plain flour, sifted

¼ cup almond meal

berries of choice and powdered sugar, to serve

Crème Anglaise

1¼ cups low-fat milk

1 vanilla bean, or 1 teaspoon vanilla extract

3 large egg yolks

⅓ cup sugar

Preheat oven to 350°F. Grease a 9-inch springform cake pan.

To make cake, beat together the egg yolks and sugar until light and creamy. Lightly whisk in the lemon rind, oil, and wine. Sift together the flour and almond meal and fold through mixture until just combined. Beat the egg whites until stiff and fold through lightly. Spoon into prepared pan and bake for 25 minutes.

Reduce heat to 325°F and bake a further 15–20 minutes. Turn off the oven, cover cake with parchment paper, and allow to rest in oven for 10 minutes. The cake will sink in the center. Remove cake from pan and cool on a wire rack or serve warm from the oven, dusted with powdered sugar, and scattered with berries. Spoon the Crème Anglaise around the outside.

To make the Crème Anglaise, heat the milk and vanilla, but don't allow to boil. In a separate bowl, beat the egg yolks and sugar until light and creamy. Gradually whisk the hot milk into the egg mixture. Heat in a double saucepan or bain-marie, stirring constantly with a whisk, until mixture thickens and coats the back of a spoon. Remove vanilla bean, if using, and transfer the mixture to a bowl. Cover and refrigerate until ready to use. This mixture can be refrigerated for up to 3 days.

Cardamom-Scented Orange Salad

Serves 4

145 calories per serving; **3.5 g** total fat; **0.2 g** saturated fat; **20 mg** sodium

4 large firm navel oranges (or Valencia if
  out of season)

1 tablespoon orange-flower water

1 tablespoon sugar

1 teaspoon cardamom seeds
  (or 4–5 cardamom pods, split)

6–8 fresh mint leaves

4 dates, pitted and sliced

2 tablespoons flaked almonds, toasted

Honey Yogurt

⅓ cup low-fat yogurt

few drops vanilla extract

1–2 teaspoons honey, gently warmed to
  soften

Peel and slice the oranges. Arrange in a layer in a flat bowl and sprinkle with the orange-flower water, sugar, and cardamom seeds. Cover and refrigerate overnight.

Combine the yogurt, vanilla, and honey in a small bowl and mix well.

To serve, remove cardamom seeds and place orange slices on plates.

Scatter with the mint, dates, and almonds and serve with the honey yogurt.

Champagne and Watermelon Jello

Serves 6 adults

130 calories per serving; **0.1 g** total fat; **0 g** saturated fat; **25 mg** sodium

1½ tablespoon gelatin

⅓ cup superfine sugar

½ cup water

2½ cups sparkling wine or champagne

1 cup puréed watermelon

Combine gelatin, sugar, and water in a saucepan and stir over low heat until sugar dissolves. Take care not to let mixture boil. Remove from heat and add the champagne and watermelon. Pour into one large serving bowl or individual cups and refrigerate until jello has set.

Gelato Duo—Watermelon and Pistachio

Serves 4

430 calories per serving; **23 g** total fat; **4.1 g** saturated fat; **80 mg** sodium

Ice cream is one of the world's favorite desserts and with this low-fat recipe you can indulge freely. The list of substitutes for the watermelon is endless: try any other kind of melon, such as honeydew, or berries, such as raspberry, blueberry, young berry, strawberry, or gooseberry. You could also choose fruits such as persimmon, lychee, nectarine, peach, apricot, cherry, mango, plum, rambutan, banana, guava, fig, kiwi, passionfruit, pineapple, or pawpaw.

Base mix for each gelato
- 2 cups skim or low-fat milk
- 4 egg yolks
- ½ cup superfine sugar

Watermelon gelato
- 2 cups puréed fresh watermelon

Pistachio gelato
- ½ cup pistachios, finely ground, or try hazelnuts, plus extra chopped pistachios, to serve

To make the base, heat the milk until near boiling point but don't boil. Beat the egg yolks and sugar in a large bowl until thick and creamy. Add a few spoons of the hot milk while beating, then gradually add the remainder in a thin stream. Transfer mixture to a double boiler or bain-marie and cook, whisking until mixture coats the back of a spoon. Don't allow the custard to boil. Pour into a jug, cover, and chill. This can be kept for a few days before making gelato.

Pour mixture into an ice-cream maker—after 1–2 minutes churning, add either the watermelon or ground pistacchio nuts, and make the gelato following manufacturer's instructions.

If you don't own an ice-cream maker, beat the custard and flavoring together, pour into ice cube trays, and freeze. Transfer to a food processor and beat well to break up the crystals then pour into an ice-cream tray. When nearly frozen, beat again then repeat this process 3–4 times over the next 1–2 hours to make as smooth as possible.

Serve with extra chopped pistachios.

Free-Form Apricot and Almond Tarts

Makes 8 tarts

310 calories per serving; **10 g** total fat; **1.1 g** saturated fat; **330 mg** sodium

When apricots are in season, these tarts may be made with the fresh variety. Make sure they're entirely ripe and juicy. Nectarines may be substituted.

Almond paste is a classic component for tarts, in particular fruit tarts. Not only does it contribute fantastic flavor with great depth, the layer between the pastry and the fruit ensures that the pastry does not become soggy during baking.

16-ounce can apricots in natural juice

Bases

2 ½ cups self-rising flour

2 tablespoons sugar

½ cup low-fat apricot or plain yogurt

½ cup low-fat milk

2 tablespoons light olive or canola oil

Almond Paste

1 egg white, lightly beaten

½ cup ground almonds

2 tablespoons sugar, plus

1–2 teaspoons extra

few drops almond extract

Preheat oven to 350°F.

Drain the apricots well and dice.

To make the bases, sift the flour and sugar into a bowl. Whisk together the yogurt, milk, and oil and pour into the flour. Mix quickly and lightly to a soft dough. Turn onto a floured board and knead gently until smooth. Wrap in plastic and refrigerate 10 minutes.

Reserve 1 tablespoon of the egg white. Combine the remainder with the almonds, sugar, and extract and mix to a paste.

To make tarts, roll the dough to ⅕-inch thickness and cut into 6-inch rounds. Place a spoon of the paste on the center of each disc and spread out, leaving a 1-inch border. Top with a spoonful of the apricots. Bring dough edges over the apricots, pleating the edges and pinching to hold in place. Brush with reserved egg white and sprinkle with extra sugar. Bake on parchment paper lined baking sheets for 15–20 minutes or until golden brown.

Chilled Fruit Gazpacho with Frozen Banana Crème

Serves 8

155 calories per serving; **0 g** total fat; **0 g** saturated fat; **25 mg** sodium

Try your own creation with this versatile dessert. Kids might like it with sparkling apple juice—let them choose and chop the fruit. For a special dinner party, try red or white wine as the liquid.

4 cups grape or apple juice

2 cups water

¼ cup superfine sugar

1 cinnamon stick or 3 star anise

zest of ½ lemon

zest of ½ orange

½ cup frozen or fresh raspberries or other berries

4 cups chopped seasonal fruit (such as kiwi fruit, pineapple, grapes, watermelon, strawberries, or other berries)

fresh mint leaves, for garnish

Frozen Banana Crème

2 large bananas, peeled and frozen

¼ cup low-fat fruit yogurt

fresh mint leaves, for garnish

To make soup, place the juice, water, sugar, cinnamon, and zests in a large stainless steel saucepan. Bring to a boil, lower heat, and simmer gently until mixture has reduced by about half or is starting to become syrupy. Strain and allow to cool. Purée with the raspberries. Divide chopped fruit among serving bowls and spoon over the syrup.

Just before serving, place the frozen bananas in a food processor with the yogurt and pulse on and off until smooth. Place a spoon of the mixture on the top of each 'soup' with a few slivers or a leaf of mint and serve immediately, before the bananas have a chance to melt.

Green Tea Mousse with Sweet Wonton Crisps

Makes 10 serves

135 calories per serving; **4 g** total fat; **2.2 g** saturated fat; **85 mg** sodium

I've chosen normal evaporated milk in this recipe rather than the reduced-fat variety, because it holds a better froth. It still makes a fairly low-fat dessert compared to its cream counterparts.

2 cups very strong Japanese or Jasmine Green Tea (you'll need about 8 tea bags)

½ cup superfine sugar

2 ½ tablespoon gelatin

1 ½ cups canned evaporated milk (see note)

1 teaspoon vanilla extract

few drops green food coloring (optional)

Wonton Crisps

6 wonton wrappers, 7 ½ by 7 ½ inches

1 egg white, lightly beaten

2 tablespoons superfine sugar

1 tablespoon almond or hazelnut meal (optional)

Place the tea, half the sugar, and gelatin in a saucepan and heat without boiling until sugar dissolves. Remove from heat. Using electric beaters, whip the evaporated milk until soft peaks form, gradually add the remaining sugar, vanilla, and coloring and beat until sugar has dissolved. Turn to a slow speed and gradually pour in the tea mixture, beating until just incorporated. Allow to sit for 10 minutes, banging a few times on the counter to break up any large air bubbles. Pour into one large glass bowl or individual glasses and refrigerate until set. Serve with a wonton crisp.

To make Wonton Crisps, brush one side lightly with the egg and dust with the sugar and nut meal. Cut in half, diagonally, and place on a lined baking sheet. Bake in a moderate oven until crisp and golden, about 10–15 minutes. Store in an airtight container.

Pineapple and Mint Sushi

Serves 6

295 calories per serving; **4.5 g** total fat; **0.7 g** saturated fat; **25 mg** sodium

This recipe is a little challenging but fun to make and well worth the effort. A real treat for guests. I love it with the Crème Anglaise on page 122 but for a fresh twist try using mint leaves instead of a vanilla bean.

1 cup calrose, arborio, or jasmine rice

1 cup low-fat milk

¾ cup water

2 tablespoons superfine sugar

1 vanilla bean or 1 teaspoon vanilla extract

2 tablespoons pineapple or apple juice

8 sheets confectioner's rice paper
  (see note on page 154)

1 bunch mint, large tender leaves
  picked and washed

½ pineapple, cut into long thin strips

¼ cup lightly toasted almonds, finely crushed

Place rice in a large saucepan, cover with cold water, and swish vigorously with your hands. Drain and repeat process until water runs clear. Allow to stand for 10–20 minutes. Combine rice, milk, water, sugar, and vanilla in a saucepan. Cover and bring to a boil, reduce heat and simmer for 5 minutes, then remove from heat, and allow to steam for 20 minutes with the lid on. Don't be tempted to remove the lid during process. Remove vanilla bean.

Using a spatula or flat wooden spoon, cut through the rice with a slicing motion while gradually adding the juice. Fan the rice at the same time to cool it down. The rice should now be quite creamy and solid. Cover with a damp cloth and keep at room temperature.

This next stage needs to be done quickly, as the rice paper softens easily, so make sure you have the fruit already sliced. On a sheet of parchment paper, place 2 sheets of rice paper on top of each other, with the long side facing you. Slide the top sheet away from you 2 inches, so there is an over-lap of about 4 inches in the middle. Place a quarter of the rice mixture along the overlapped area, pressing down gently as you would for sushi. Lay mint leaves down the center then top with a line of the pineapple. Bring closest edge of rice paper over the rice, then roll up to make a firm log, using the parchment paper to help roll it tightly. Cover tightly in plastic wrap and refrigerate until ready to serve.

To serve, sprinkle almonds over a flat board or sheet of parchment paper. Remove plastic from sushi and roll in almonds to coat. Cut diagonally in desired lengths and serve as is, with a fruit purée, or even Lime Mint Sauce on page 136.

Warm Tropical Fruit Salad with Orange Rum Sauce

Serves 4

220 calories per serving; **1.5 g** total fat; **0.1 g** saturated fat; **10 mg** sodium

Try with a dollop of thick yogurt or a little shredded coconut.

2 bananas, halved lengthwise

2 teaspoons lemon juice

1 mango, sliced

4 slices pineapple, halved and cored

1 tablespoon brown sugar

1 teaspoon cinnamon

oil for brushing pan

Orange Rum Sauce

¾ cup orange juice

2 tablespoons rum

2 tablespoons brown sugar

Brush the banana with the lemon juice, then toss all the fruit in the sugar and cinnamon. Set aside.

To make the Orange Rum Sauce, combine the orange juice, rum, and brown sugar in a small saucepan and bring to a boil. Reduce heat and simmer until the mixture thickens to a sauce consistency, about 15 minutes. Keep warm.

Heat a nonstick pan over medium-low heat and brush with oil. Add the fruit and cook 2–3 minutes on each side or until golden brown and heated through. Serve with the sauce spooned over.

Berry and Apple Pastries

Makes 8 pieces

130 calories per serving; **3 g** total fat; **0.6 g** saturated fat; **125 mg** sodium

Try sprinkling this with a little mixed powdered sugar and cocoa just before serving.

3 cups fresh diced apples and mixed berries—try strawberries, raspberries, or blueberries

2 tablespoons ground roasted hazelnuts

1 tablespoon liqueur of choice or orange-flower water

2 tablespoons cocoa

2 tablespoons superfine sugar

8 sheets filo pastry

Fruit Custard

½ cup low-fat custard

¼ cup fruit purée—try mango or raspberry

Preheat the oven to 400°F.

Mix the fruit with the ground nuts and liqueur. In a separate bowl, combine the cocoa and sugar.

Lay a sheet of filo pastry on a clean dry surface and dust lightly with the cocoa mixture. Top with another sheet and dust again. Repeat with another 2 sheets leaving the top sheet undusted. Cut the pastry stack into 4 crosswise.

Divide fruit mixture between pastries, laying it down one short side and leaving 1 inch at each end. Roll up into fingers, tucking in the ends. Repeat process with remaining pastry and fruit. Place on a parchment paper-lined baking sheet and bake for 8–10 minutes or until golden brown.

Combine the custard and fruit purée. Serve pastries on flat plates with the custard spooned around the outside.

Banana and Mango Clafouti

Serves 4

365 calories per serving; **6.5 g** total fat; **3.2 g** saturated fat; **105 mg** sodium

2 large ripe bananas, sliced lengthwise

2 teaspoons lemon juice

¼ cup brown sugar

2 tablespoons cornstarch

2 tablespoons brandy

2 mangoes, sliced

Topping

¼ cup sugar, plus 1 tablespoon extra

2 tablespoons flour

2 eggs

½ cup ricotta cheese

¼ cup low-fat milk

1 teaspoon vanilla extract

Preheat oven to 400ºF.

Mix the banana with the lemon juice, sugar, cornstarch, and brandy. Place half in a single layer in 4 lightly oiled ovenproof dishes or one large dish. Top with a layer of the mango and finish with the remaining banana.

To make the topping, place the sugar, flour, eggs, ricotta, milk, and vanilla in a blender and blend until smooth. Pour over the fruit and bake for 25–30 minutes or until set and lightly browned. Sprinkle with extra sugar and place under a hot broiler for 1–2 minutes or until browned. Serve while hot.

Papaya and Kiwi Compote with Lime Mint Sauce

Serves 6

120 calories per serving (includes yogurt); **2 g** total fat; **1.1 g** saturated fat; **40 mg** sodium

Papaya seeds are great for digestion, so set a few aside. When puréed they add a lovely sharp, peppery touch to savory dressings.

1 papaya

6 kiwi fruit

¼ cup thick natural yogurt, to serve (optional)

Lime Mint Sauce

juice of 1 lime

1 teaspoon grated lime zest

¼ cup water

2 tablespoons superfine sugar

¼ cup chopped mint

To make the Lime Mint Sauce, heat the lime juice, zest, water, and sugar in a small saucepan and cook over a low heat until the sugar dissolves. Cook for 5 minutes, then cool and purée with the mint leaves.

Remove the seeds from the papaya (see note). Peel and slice both fruits and arrange on plates or a platter. Drizzle with the Lime Mint Sauce and serve plain or with thick natural yogurt.

Orange and Pecan Biscotti (page 140)

baking

Orange and Pecan Biscotti

Makes 30 biscotti

70 calories per serving; **2.5 g** total fat; **0.3 g** saturated fat; **15 mg** sodium

1¾ cups plain flour

½ teaspoon baking powder

2 large eggs

½ cup superfine sugar

1 teaspoon vanilla extract

2 teaspoons grated orange rind

¾ cup pecan nuts

egg white, for brushing

Preheat oven to 350ºF.

Sift the flour and baking powder into a large bowl. Set aside. Using electric mixers, beat the eggs and sugar until thick and doubled in bulk. Beat in the vanilla and orange rind. Gently fold into the flour, together with the pecans. Transfer to a well-floured board and knead gently until smooth. Divide in quarters and shape each into an 8-inch log. Lay on parchment paper-lined baking sheets, brush with egg white and bake for 15–20 minutes or until golden brown and firm. Allow to cool for 10 minutes, then slice diagonally into ½-inch slices.

Turn oven down to 325ºF.

Lay biscuits flat on baking sheets and bake for 20–25 minutes or until dry and crisp. Cool on a wire rack before storing in an airtight container.

Guinness Fruit Cake

Makes a 12-inch loaf or a 10-inch round cake

285 calories per serving; **9 g** total fat; **1.2 g** saturated fat; **245 mg** sodium

1 cup Guinness stout

¾ cup molasses or treacle

1 teaspoon baking soda

1 tablespoon grated ginger

1½ cups mixed dried fruit

2 cups self-rising flour

2 teaspoons mixed spice

3 eggs

¾ cup brown sugar

½ cup light olive or canola oil

Preheat oven to 350ºF. Grease and line a loaf or cake pan with parchment paper.

In a large saucepan, bring the stout and molasses to a boil (take care as it foams up). Remove from the heat, add the baking soda, ginger, and dried fruit. Cover and allow mixture to cool to room temperature.

Combine the flour and mixed spice.

In a large bowl, beat the eggs and sugar until thick and creamy. Gradually add the oil while beating. Gently fold the beer and flour mixtures alternately into the eggs, ending with the flour. Spoon mixture into prepared pan and bake for 1 hour or until a skewer inserted in the center comes out clean and cake springs back when touched. Allow to cool in pan for 10 minutes before turning on to a wire rack.

Guinness Fruit Cake

Fresh Rhubarb and Buttermilk Cake

Makes a 10-inch cake

360 calories per serving; **7 g** total fat; **1.1 g** saturated fat; **230 mg** sodium

This cake is delicious just plain iced, but its slight pudding consistency also makes it ideal as a warm dessert served with the reserved syrup.

Although people think of rhubarb as a fruit, it is actually a vegetable. Its leaves are poisonous—they contain oxalic acid —and should be removed as soon as you bring the bunch home.

3 cups chopped rhubarb
½ cup water
½ cup orange juice
1 cup sugar
3 eggs
¼ cup oil
½ cup well-shaken buttermilk
2½ cups self-rising flour
1 teaspoon ginger

Buttermilk and Orange Icing
2 cups powdered sugar
grated rind of ½ orange
1 teaspoon orange juice
2–3 tablespoons well-shaken buttermilk

Preheat oven to 350°F. Lightly oil and flour a 10-inch cake pan.

Combine the rhubarb, water, juice, and half of the sugar in a saucepan and bring to a boil. Reduce heat and simmer for 10 minutes, until rhubarb is tender. Allow to cool in liquid. Strain, reserving liquid. Mash rhubarb, adding back enough liquid to measure 1½ cups purée.

If there is any remaining liquid, it can be boiled to reduce and thicken, and served as a syrup with the cake, if desired (see note).

With electric mixers beat the eggs with the remaining ½ cup sugar until thick and creamy. Gradually add the oil and buttermilk, while beating. Sift together the flour and ginger and gently fold ⅓ through the batter. Fold through half of the rhubarb, then repeat, so flour is the last addition. Spoon into prepared pan and bake for 35 minutes or until a toothpick inserted into the center comes out clean.

To make icing, beat together the powdered sugar, orange juice, and enough buttermilk to make a spreadable consistency. Spread on the cake when cool.

Hazelnut and Ginger Meringues

Makes about 48 meringues

60 calories per meringue; **4 g** total fat; **0.2 g** saturated fat; **5 mg** sodium

1 cup roughly chopped roasted hazelnuts

1¼ cups superfine sugar

3 egg whites

pinch of cream of tartar

2 teaspoons finely diced glace ginger

1 teaspoon ginger powder

48 whole raw hazelnuts

Preheat oven to 250°F.

Combine the chopped hazelnuts and ¼ cup of the superfine sugar in a food processor until finely chopped. In a separate bowl beat the egg whites and cream of tartar until soft peaks form.

Gradually beat in the remaining cup of sugar until sugar has dissolved and mixture is stiff. Fold in the hazelnut and sugar mixture and the glace and powdered ginger.

Place heaped teaspoons of mixture on baking sheets lined with parchment paper, allowing room for spreading, and top each with a whole hazelnut. Bake for 40–45 minutes or until dry and crisp, but not browned.

Oat Bars

Makes 24 bars

105 calories per serving; **3.5 g** total fat; **0.6 g** saturated fat; **20 mg** sodium

3 cups rolled oats

1 cup finely diced dried apricots or peaches

¾ cup sugar

⅓ cup slivered almonds

1 teaspoon cinnamon

¼ cup water

½ cup low-fat apricot yogurt

2 tablespoons melted margarine

1 tablespoon sesame seeds

Preheat oven to 375°F. Line a 11 by 7-inch rectangular pan with parchment paper.

Combine the oats, apricots, sugar, almonds, and cinnamon in a bowl. Lightly beat the water, yogurt, and margarine, pour over, and mix well to combine. This can also be mixed in a food processor, but don't overbeat.

Press mixture into prepared pan, sprinkle with sesame seeds and mark into 24 bars. Bake for 20 minutes or until crisp and golden-brown. Cool in pan on a wire rack, then store in an airtight container for up to 2 weeks. Suitable for freezing.

Lemongrass and Lime Sponge Cake

Makes a 9-inch cake

265 calories per serving; **5 g** total fat; **2.4 g** saturated fat; **210 mg** sodium

Ground lemongrass can be found in most supermarkets. If you can't find it, chop 1 tablespoon fresh lemongrass very finely and boil for 10 minutes in a ½ cup water. Allow to steep for 10 minutes, strain, and use this as the hot water for the sponge mix.

Fresh lemongrass is often found in Thai dishes. The bottom part of the stem is only used, and the first few layers are removed to reveal the tender core. The core is very thinly sliced and added to salads, or bruised to release flavors and pounded in a mortar to be added to curry pastes.

3 eggs, separated
¾ cup superfine sugar
1 teaspoon grated lime zest
1 cup self-rising flour
1 teaspoon ground lemongrass (see note)
3 tablespoons hot water

Lime Cream
½ cup low-fat ricotta cheese
⅓ cup light cream cheese
¾ cup powdered sugar
grated zest of ½ lime
1 teaspoon lime juice

Preheat oven to 350°F. Grease and flour a 9-inch cake pan.

Beat the egg whites until stiff peaks form. Gradually add the sugar and continue beating until dissolved. Add the yolks and lime zest and beat just to combine. Sift together the flour and lemongrass and gently fold through the egg mixture followed by the water.

Spoon mixture into prepared pan and bake for 20–25 minutes or until golden and cake springs back when pressed gently. Leave in pan for 5–10 minutes before turning onto a wire rack to cool. Cut sponge cake in half and fill with the lime cream. Sprinkle top with powdered sugar.

To make Lime Cream, place all ingredients in a bowl and beat with an electric mixer until thick and creamy.

Bush Bread with Australian Dukkah

Makes 12 large wedges and 1 cup of dukkah

Bread: 110 calories per serving; **2.5 g** total fat; **0.6 g** saturated fat; **175 mg** sodium

Dukkah: 75 calories per cup; **8 g** total fat; **0.9 g** saturated fat; **0 mg** sodium

The herbs in this recipe are native to Australia. They are gradually becoming available outside of Australia. Meditteranean dukkah usually uses cilantro, cumin, sesame seeds, and hazelnuts, so if you're reluctant to try the Australian version, give that one a go.

Bread

2 cups self-rising flour

1 tablespoon wattle seeds (or linseed)

1 teaspoon lemon myrtle

1 teaspoon freshly ground pepper

1 cup well-shaken buttermilk

1 tablespoon macadamia or olive oil

milk for brushing dough

Dukkah Mixture

½ cup chopped macadamia nuts

¼ cup chopped hazelnuts

1 tablespoon ground dried tomato

1 teaspoon lemon myrtle

1 teaspoon freshly ground pepper

1 teaspoon aniseed

Preheat oven to 350°F.

Sift the flour and seasonings into a large bowl and make a well in the center. Combine the buttermilk and oil and pour into the center. Mix quickly and lightly to a soft dough, then turn onto a floured board and knead until smooth. Shape into a round loaf shape and place on a lined or lightly oiled baking sheet. Brush with milk and bake for 40–50 minutes or until golden brown and hollow sounding when tapped. Serve with macadamia or extra virgin olive oil and the Dukkah for dipping.

To make Dukkah Mixture, place chopped macadamia nuts and chopped hazelnuts on a roasting pan and bake in a moderate oven until golden brown. Grind, then toss with ground tomato, lemon myrtle, pepper, and aniseed. Return to oven and bake until mixture becomes aromatic. This can also be done on the stove top in a nonstick pan, but take care not to burn the herb mixture. This can be stored in an airtight container for 1–2 weeks, or longer in the freezer. Try sprinkling on salads, steamed rice, pasta, and meat or fish dishes for a tasty touch.

Raisin and Currant Tea Bread

Makes a 9-inch round cake or a 9 by 5-inch loaf

155 calories per serving; **2.5 g** total fat; **0.3 g** saturated fat; **115 mg** sodium

This is delicious either plain or spread with fresh ricotta cheese.

1 cup raisins

1½ cup currants

1½ cups cold strong Earl Grey or Lady Grey tea

1 tablespoon treacle

1 egg, lightly beaten

¾ cup brown sugar

2 cups self-rising flour, sifted

1 teaspoon mixed spice

½ cup walnuts

Place the fruits in a large bowl, pour over the tea, and stir in the treacle. Cover and allow to soak overnight.

Preheat oven to 325ºF and line a 9-inch cake pan with parchment paper.

Stir beaten egg into fruit mixture followed by the sugar, then the sifted flour, spice, and walnuts. Spoon into prepared pan and bake for 1–1¼ hours or until a toothpick inserted in the center comes out clean. Allow to cool for 10 minutes in pan on a wire rack before turning out.

Chocolate and Orange Cake

Makes 12 regular muffins, or a 9-inch cake

225 calories per muffin; **13 g** total fat; **2.5 g** saturated fat; **130 mg** sodium

3 eggs

½ cup firmly packed brown sugar

⅓ cup olive oil

½ cup mashed baking apple (or cooked apple purée)

1 tablespoon grated orange zest

1 cup self-rising flour

½ cup almond meal

½ cup cocoa

⅓ cup well-shaken buttermilk

powdered sugar, for dusting (optional)

Preheat the oven to 350ºF. Lightly oil or spray the muffin pans or the cake pan.

Beat the eggs and sugar with electric beaters until thick and creamy. Gradually add the oil while beating, followed by the apple and grated zest. Sift together the flour, almond meal, and cocoa and lightly fold half through the batter. Stir in the buttermilk, then fold through the remaining flour mixture until just combined. Spoon into prepared muffin pans or cake pan, and bake for 15–20 minutes for the muffins, or 35–40 minutes for the cake, or until a toothpick inserted in the center comes out clean. Allow to cool in the pans for 10 minutes before turning out on a wire rack to cool completely. If preferred, dust with powdered sugar before serving.

Pistachio and Carrot Cake

Makes a 9 by 9-inch square cake

310 calories per serving; **9.5 g** total fat; **1.7 g** saturated fat; **235 mg** sodium

You may have noticed a lot of nuts used in this book. Many people don't realize that all nuts are healthy.

They contain valuable nutrients and the oils are mainly monounsaturated or polyunsaturated, the preferred type for good health. I often use nuts to replace some of the texture and flavor lost when creating low-fat recipes—they add a lot of interest to a recipe. Be creative and experiment with your favorite nuts. The only caution: if you are watching your weight, use nuts instead of other fats, not in addition to.

2 cups self-rising flour

½ cup wholemeal self-rising flour

½ teaspoon baking soda

1 teaspoon cinnamon

1 teaspoon nutmeg

½ cup raisins

¾ cup roughly chopped unsalted roasted pistachio nuts, or preferred nuts (see note)

1½ cups grated carrot

½ cup brown sugar

⅓ cup canola oil

2 eggs

½ cup well-shaken buttermilk

½ pound crushed pineapple, drained

Icing

2 cups powdered sugar, sifted

¼ cup light cream cheese

2 teaspoons grated lemon rind

1 teaspoon lemon juice

Preheat oven to 350°F. Lightly oil and flour, or line a 9 by-9 inch square cake pan with parchment paper.

Sift the flours, soda, and spices into a large bowl. Toss through the raisins, nuts, and carrot. In a separate bowl, beat the sugar and oil until light and fluffy. While still beating, add the eggs, one at a time, beating well after each addition, then stir in the buttermilk. Pour into the flour mixture with the pineapple and stir lightly to make a batter.

Spoon into prepared pan and bake for 25–35 minutes or until a toothpick inserted in the center comes out clean. Allow to cool for 10 minutes in pan before turning onto a wire rack to cool. When cold, spread with icing and, if desired, decorate with finely chopped pistachios.

To make icing, place all ingredients in a bowl and mix well. Gradually add a little boiling water a few drops at a time, to bring to spreading consistency.

Citrus Panforte

Makes about 40 pieces

70 calories per serving; **4.5 g** total fat; **0.4 g** saturated fat; **0 mg** sodium

Confectioner's rice paper can be found in most health food stores, European delicatessens, and well-stocked supermarkets. Don't confuse it with the Asian rice paper.

confectioner's rice paper for lining pan
  (see note)
1 cup almonds
1 cup walnuts or macadamia nuts
grated zest of 1 lemon
grated zest of 1 orange
½ cup glace ginger (or preferred glace fruit)
1 tablespoon grated orange rind
1 teaspoon grated lemon rind
1 teaspoon ground cinnamon
1 teaspoon mixed spice
pinch ground white pepper
½ cup plain flour
½ cup honey
⅓ cup sugar
powdered sugar (optional)

Preheat oven to 350°F. Line the base of a 8 by 8 by 1½-inch square pan with the rice paper, and line the sides of the pan with parchment paper.

Combine the nuts, zests, ginger, rinds, spices, and flour in a large bowl. Mix well.

Warm the honey and sugar in a saucepan over low heat until the sugar dissolves, brushing down sides of pan with a brush dipped in hot water to stop sugar sticking. Bring to a boil, reduce heat, and simmer for 6–8 minutes or until mixture forms a soft ball when dropped in a glass of cold water. Immediately mix through the fruit mixture, stirring well, to combine thoroughly.

Spoon into prepared pan and flatten top, pushing mixture out to the edges. Bake for 30–35 minutes. Allow to cool in pan on a wire rack. When cool, cut into squares and dust with powdered sugar if desired.

Sweet Potato Wedges

Makes 10 wedges

195 calories per serving; **5.5 g** total fat; **2.3 g** saturated fat; **255 mg** sodium

2 cups self-rising flour
1 teaspoon mixed spice
¾ cup cold mashed sweet potato
  (the orange variety)
1 tablespoon brown sugar
½ cup low-fat milk
1 tablespoon canola or light olive oil
low-fat milk, extra, for brushing

Apricot Ricotta Whip

1 cup fresh ricotta cheese
1 teaspoon vanilla extract
½ cup dried apricots, soaked for
  1 hour to soften, drained, and chopped
1 tablespoon powdered sugar

Preheat oven to 375°F. Lightly oil or spray a baking sheet or line with parchment paper.

Sift the flour and mixed spice into a large bowl. In a separate bowl or blender, beat together the mashed sweet potato, sugar, milk, and oil until smooth. Pour into the flour and mix quickly and lightly with a butter knife to a soft dough. Turn on to a floured board and knead gently until smooth. Shape into a 9-inch circle and place on prepared tray. Mark into wedges and brush top with milk. Bake for 20 minutes or until golden brown. Serve warm or cold with the apricot ricotta whip.

To make apricot ricotta whip, beat all the ingredients together until light and fluffy with electric beaters or in a food processor.

focus on flavor

Everyone wants to get pleasure from the food they eat, so

there's no point in changing the way you eat if you're not

going to enjoy it. If you simply want to start eating better for

your long-term health, and still enjoy the great pleasures

food has to offer, remember that flavor, along with visual

appeal and texture, are so very important. Life is too short to

go on bland, uninteresting diets.

Here are a few ideas to help you liven up your meals.

from the east

rice wine vinegar For a light, clean flavor that adds mild acidity. Adds a lift to rice, salads, Asian-style marinades, or splash on fish.

mirin A blend of rice wine and sugar that adds a subtle sweetness and bouquet to dishes, dressings, stir-fries, and marinades.

sesame oil Just a few drops are all that's needed to add a rich and aromatic flavor to dishes. Great in marinades, stir-fries, and just tossed through rice, or in salad dressings. It is powerful, though, so go a drop at a time or dilute in milder oils or vinegar.

fish sauce For a fresh, aromatic touch of the sea, only a splash is needed. Add to stocks or the cooking liquid for Asian soups. It's high in salt, though, so go easy if you're watching your sodium intake.

kaffir lime leaves This ingredient adds a pungent, lime-like aura when added to the cooking liquid of rice, soups, noodles, ravioli. Also use crumbled in casseroles and baked fish or chicken dishes.

hoisin and oyster sauce A change from the usual soy, hoisin is sweet and spicy and great as a glaze or marinade. Oyster sauce is made from oyster water and salt and adds a rich, characteristic element to dishes. Both are fairly high in salt—look for the ones without MSG.

dried mushrooms For a rich, smoky mushroom flavor, add to cooking water of soups, rice, noodles, or just soak to soften and toss through stir-fries and salads.

ginger An indispensable ingredient that is not only good for your health, but incredibly versatile—from the fresh root chopped in stir-fries, to pickled for sushi, or tossed through salads, rice, or sauces, or even the piquant glazed ginger for adding zing to cakes and baking.

lemongrass An aromatic, citrus flavor for a huge range of dishes. Try lemongrass chopped fresh, dried, preserved or even ground.

wasabi If sinus-clearing heat is what you're after, use it in abundance. For a more subtle, fresh bite to sauces, rice or spreads, use just a touch of this Japanese horseradish.

from the west

balsamic vinegar A rich, dark, and slightly sweet vinegar used for centuries by Italians in salad dressings, marinades, glazes, splashed over fish, and meat, or just added to olive oil for dipping bread.

extra virgin olive oil Loaded with the valuable monounsaturates, olive oil may be high in fat, as all oils are, but a good-quality, fruity extra virgin olive oil will go a long way and bring a wonderful aromatic flavor to food cooked in it or salads dressed with it. It's well worth the investment on your health and pleasure and one of the healthiest things to have with your bread.

nut oils Macadamia, hazelnut, walnut, and other nut oils all have a distinctive flavor and can add a new dimension to your cooking. Taste and experiment for yourself.

tomato paste Look for the one with no added salt as, being concentrated, the natural salt of the tomato speaks for itself. Add to cold or hot pasta sauces, dressings, and rice dishes. Tomato paste also adds a rich, full element to low-fat stews and casseroles, or when added to meat or onion when sautéeing and allowed to turn a rust color and become aromatic.

mustard Whether wholegrain, Dijon, hot English, honey, or any of the huge range available, mustard adds a distinct flavor and richness to sandwiches, dressings, or spread over meat and roasts. It's fairly high in salt.

fresh herbs There's nothing that gives dishes quite the lift that fresh herbs do. Experiment to find your own favorite food-and-herb combinations, whether tossed through salad, sauces, pasta, rice, soup, as a "crust" for fish and meat, or just chopped and added to a simple sandwich.

nuts and seeds Another food abounding in monounsaturated and polyunsaturated oils. Use as a crunchy surprise in texture and flavor in salads, sandwiches, through rice and pasta, ground or chopped on meat, or through breads and cakes. For extra flavor and richness, toast or dry roast before using.

measurements and conversions

imperial/metric conversion chart

Metric cup and spoon sizes

Measurements used in this book refer to the standard metric cup and spoon sets approved by the Standards Association of Australia.
A basic metric cup set consists of:
1 cup, ½ cup, ⅓ cup and ¼ cup sizes.
The basic spoon set comprises 1 tablespoon, 1 teaspoon, ½ teaspoon, ¼ teaspoon.

Cup	Spoon
¼ cup = 60ml	¼ teaspoon = 1.25ml
⅓ cup = 80ml	½ teaspoon = 2.5ml
½ cup = 125ml	1 teaspoon = 5ml
1 cup = 250ml	1 tablespoon = 20ml

Liquids

Imperial	Metric	Metric
1fl oz	-	30 ml
2fl oz	¼ cup	60ml
3fl oz	-	100ml
4fl oz	½ cup	125ml
5fl oz	-	150ml
6fl oz	¾ cup	200ml
8fl oz	1 cup	250ml
10fl oz	1¼ cups	300ml
12fl oz	1½ cups	375ml
14 fl oz	1¾ cups	425ml
15fl oz	-	475ml
16fl oz	2 cups	500ml
20fl oz (1 pint)	2½ cups	600ml

Mass (weight)

(Approximate conversion for cookery purposes)

Imperial	Metric	Imperial	Metric
½oz	15g	10oz	315g
1oz	30g	11oz	345g
2oz	60g	12oz (¾ lb)	375g
3oz	90g	13oz	410g
4oz (¼ lb)	125g	14oz	440g
5oz	155g	15oz	470g
6oz	185g	16oz (1lb)	500g (0.5kg)
7oz	220g	24oz (1½ lb)	750g
8oz (½ lb)	250g	32oz (2lb)	1000g (1kg)
9oz	280g	3lb	1500g (1.5kg)

Oven temperatures

Oven	Fahrenheit	Celsius
Very slow	250°	120°
Slow	275–300°	140–150°
Moderately slow	325°	160°
Moderate	350°	180°
Moderately hot	375°	190°
Hot	400–450°	200–230°
Very hot	475–500°	250–260°

Note: For fan ovens set approximately 20° Celsius below the stated temperature.

index